People Management in the 21st Century

Understanding the Basics

by
Maurice O'Connell

The Key to Understanding and Developing your
own and your Teams true Potential

authorHOUSE®

AuthorHouse™ UK Ltd.
500 Avebury Boulevard
Central Milton Keynes, MK9 2BE
www.authorhouse.co.uk
Phone: 08001974150

First published by AuthorHouse 5/10/2007

ISBN: 978-1-4343-0436-0 (sc)

Printed in the United States of America
Bloomington, Indiana

This book is printed on acid-free paper.

Cover Design: © Cesair - www.istockphoto.com

DISCLAIMER:

YOU AGREE THAT THE AUTHOR, PUBLISHER AND THEIR AGENTS ARE NOT RESPONSIBLE OR LIABLE TO ANY PERSON OR ENTITY WHATSOEVER FOR ANY LOSS, DAMAGES (WHETHER ACTUAL, CONSEQUENTIAL OR OTHERWISE), INJURY, CLAIM, LIABILITY OR OTHER CAUSE OF ANY KIND OR CHARACTER WHATSOEVER BASED UPON OR RESULTING FROM THE USE OF INFORMATION PROVIDED WITHIN THIS BOOK.

ALL THE INFORMATION CONTAINED WITHIN THIS BOOK IS PROVIDED IN GOOD FAITH AND "AS IS" AND YOU AGREE WITH THE USE OF SUCH INFORMATION AT YOUR SOLE RISK. THE AUTHOR, PUBLISHER AND THEIR AGENTS EXPRESSLY DISCLAIM ALL WARRANTIES OF ANY KIND, WHETHER EXPRESS OR IMPLIED, INCLUDING, BUT NOT LIMITED TO THE IMPLIED WARRANTIES OF ORGANIZATIONAL, CORPORATE AND/OR PERSONAL IMPROVEMNET. WITHOUT LIMITATION, THE AUTHOR, PUBLISHER AND THEIR AGENTS MAKE NO WARRANTY THAT THE INFORMATION PROVIDED WITHIN THIS BOOK WILL MEET WITH YOUR OWN OR YOUR ORGANIZATIONS REQUIREMENTS OR EXPECTATIONS. ANY DECISIONS TAKEN AS A RESULT OF USING THE INFORMATION PROVIDED WITHIN THIS BOOK IS DONE SO AT YOUR SOLE RISK AND YOU WILL BE SOLELY RESPONSIBLE FOR THE OUTCOME FROM THE USE OF SUCH INFORMATION.

Contents

Acknowledgments

To the Managers and Directors of the various companies and organisations that I've worked with over the past twenty years, especially those who saw in me the ability and were willing to risk in me the responsibility of taking on new tasks. It is this willingness by those special few to take the risk of giving opportunities to those around them followed by their on-going support and guidance that has taught me and many others like me what good people management is all about. It is good people management skills like this that can turn everyday capable, reliable and trustworthy employees into leaders of the future. To those of you who were always willing to share their expertise and ideas and whose door was always open for advice – I thank you.

To my family who have nearly always supported my late nights and sometimes early mornings typing away at the laptop while piecing together my first publication – thank you for your patience but it may not be over.

To Dean Shah and Sasha Lee of Authorhouse (UK) and Bob DeGroff of Authorhouse (USA) who have guided me through the unknown of transforming what was once just a file on my laptop into something tangible and then making it available to the world – It would not have been possible without you and for that I am grateful.

Wherever possible, surround yourself with people who are smarter, wiser and more successful than you, but just as importantly, understand their failures and learn from their successes.

Unknown author

I've always liked the above quote and the numerous variations on it – what a pity that the originator isn't known to me so that I could give them the credit they deserve for such a profound statement.

Looking to the Future - An Introduction

The world in general seems to be surging ahead and getting progressively wealthier with an increasing number of people who are earning and spending more than ever. There will always be economic ups and downs but the world's appetite for success and better standards of living will ensure that economic growth will continue over the longer term. This general increase of world-wide wealth automatically creates the need for increased output in the construction, manufacturing, retail, services and hospitality sectors to mention just a few. This, one would imagine, should make it much easier for companies and organizations alike to not just survive but flourish with relative ease in a world with so much disposable income. This is where the paradox begins because the more businesses that are set up to cater for this glorious increase in demand the stronger the possibilities that it will automatically give rise to ever-greater competition in order for each of them to succeed at attracting what they believe to be their rightful share of the success pie. This competitiveness is without doubt excellent for consumers as it helps drive better all-round quality and lower prices but what affect does it actually have on the every-day running of a business and more importantly what is required by people at all levels of companies and organizations in order for them to deliver and maintain the need for constant improvement. The drive for efficiency and productivity is greater than ever and so is the pressure on everyone involved to ensure that targets are met and continuously improved upon.

Success in any business is down to how people within their respective company or organization work together and how successful the partnership is between employee and Team Leader regardless of what level they are at. Employees need to understand that a fair and honest days work is required as part of their contract in order for them to earn their rightful share of wage or salary. Like-wise Team Leaders at all levels must understand that they too are employees and in order for them to earn their rightful share of wage or salary they will need to find ways of maximising their own and each of their subordinate's effectiveness within the business as a whole. It's not always how hard we work that makes us successful but how smart we work and better still how smart we work when working hard.

Now that we've got this far, let me ask you a question. How is work treating you these days – is everything running smoothly? Maybe you are the one person in a million who would regard everyone and everything within your working environment as being the essence of perfection? Is it really possible that you and your work colleagues are the most productive and happiest group ever, each of you having reached your fullest potential or is it more likely the case that you are secretly wishing for some kind of change to take place in order for your working environment to become a more productive, meaningful, worthwhile and inspirational place to be. Well, I bet that's exactly what's going through your mind and furthermore I can say it with absolute certainty because no matter how small or large your organization, there will always be room for improvement and especially around the critical areas of people management and people development. If you are currently involved in or would like to be involved in the managing and developing of people as part of any growing and respected organization or business, then the ideas and tools presented here should help you in making much smarter all-round decisions which in turn will greatly increase the odds of you and your team succeeding in your working environment. The reason I say this is that I've seen so often at first hand how the ideas and tools presented here have succeeded and very often where a series of other ideas and tools have previously failed.

It is here that we explore the make-up of the successful people managers of the future and how their successful interaction with others around them will result in employees not only looking at their company or organization as being a place of work but as being a great place to work. This is quite possibly the key to all-round success for any business in the future and one which will elevate a company's standing within its own organization and throughout the business world as a whole.

Companies and organizations around the world which have in the past been voted tops by their employees as being great companies to work for have usually been the kind of companies and organizations to see a steady increase in their business and profits. The reason for this is that employees who genuinely feel that they work in a place that emanates trust, credibility, respect and fairness are without doubt working in a place where management strongly believe in such ideals and the results for both the employees and the company alike are hugely rewarding. Some of the benefits that can be seen and felt in such enlightened organizations are higher productivity, greater retention and increased innovation and creativity.

Good people management skills, good people development skills, empathy towards others, respect (if not an understanding) for all things different and sometimes a sense of humour are just some of the attributes that make some people managers stand out more than others. This can also, by default, make them the kind of leaders at work and in life that others automatically look to for guidance and assurance. The people managers of the future will not be judged on results alone but also on how they achieved those results and just as importantly the impact it had on the employees involved. The final question should be based on whether results were driven by force and fear or if the employees were informed and willing participants in a common goal.

It has happened all too often in the past that organizations and companies who were doing so well decided to go all out for efficiency and productivity but because that drive for the ultimate goal wasn't controlled and monitored in an appropriate manner they then found themselves caught up in what I call "The Mini Skirt Syndrome". The Mini Skirt Syndrome refers to any organisation's or company's determination to continuously improve on efficiency and productivity without fully understanding the possible negative consequences unfolding elsewhere within the company. Raising the bar when it comes to efficiency at work is like raising the hemline of a mini skirt. The higher it goes the more attractive the expectations and in many cases the initial results but an over-zealous, uncontrolled, unmonitored push for what may seem like the ultimate in perfection may very well lead to exposing something that may be seen as a step too far and in so doing throw your teams commitment, willingness and eagerness to work into freefall. History has continuously proved that the desired balance between achieving positive results and the appropriateness used in achieving them is what makes good results go on for longer. Efficiency, as an on-going long-term and moving goal will be better and more positively executed if management and Team Leaders at all levels continuously strive in the search for a more positive and coherent balance between the provision of appropriate working environments, the supply of proper and sufficient tools, appropriate on-going training, the encouraging of employee involvement and proactive communication between all levels of the work force. The most important factor in all of this is that is has to be practiced and driven from the top down and in so doing will help greatly in maximising the true efficiency and productivity of any business with the willingness of its employees.

The biggest asset of all for any business or organization is its people and short term gains at the employees' expense will only lead to reduced profits and a loss of credibility for the organization that would otherwise have had an opportunity to develop and expand further. It is amazing that even in the start of the 21st century how many businesses and organizations fail to understand this basic concept. Those that do understand, embrace and promote such ideals are gaining a lot of ground on their competitors and doing so with a much happier and committed work force!

When I first started out on the road to employment more than twenty years ago, I would have given anything to avail of all the knowledge and experience that has gone into this book - a combination of the absolute brilliance & common sense of some of the people I've met along the way, together with my own experiences as a result of their intervention and sometimes not. Peoples views on what is considered to be good and not-so-good styles of management have been changing and evolving with every decade for at least a century but not as significantly since more recent times and it is here that we explore the basics of what is going to be some of the most powerful, influential and effective ways of managing and developing people in the coming decades.

What I find most appealing about this refined style of people management and people development, is not alone is it more effective but it is also proving to be a lot easier, both for the manager and the employee involved – alleluia, I hear you cry.

No matter how often your people management skills need refining and they will do as time goes on, it's the appropriate basics or foundations (minus unnecessary red tape) being in place from the start that will help you in coping with almost any circumstances that may arise. It will also make your job as a Supervisor, Team Leader, Manager or Director a much less demanding task and a much more rewarding venture both for yourself and just as importantly the people who will ultimately benefit from your unique and effective wisdom and ability. Remember, you are often the link between those you report to and those that report into you, a sometimes tricky balancing act especially when trying to keep both sides of the fence happy while maintaining your own sense of professional aptitude and well being.

The successful people managers of the 21st century won't necessarily be those with university degrees alone but will most definitely be those with a unique balance between traditional educational requirements and the ability to empathise, be part of, support and motivate those that they work with. Some of the most successful individuals in the world are not necessarily academic geniuses, even though many may be, but most do have the kind of self belief, positive attitude and drive that can be emotionally infectious and encouraging to those they interact with. Acknowledging this kind of successful behaviour is one of the reasons why there is a world wide rethink on what exactly should be classed as successful people management. It is most certainly a balanced interaction between academic intelligence and emotional intelligence that drives this kind of success. It is also the reason why a redefining of the basics in people management skills and people development skills is absolutely necessary in order for them to be more effective, both for the business and the individual alike.

The overall aim of this book is to introduce some of the most powerful yet easy to use managerial tools of the future. Most of the managerial tools and ideas presented here have been designed, refined and tested successfully over several years and can easily enable Team Leaders at all levels of organizations to better understand and develop their own and their teams' current and future potential.

Maurice O'Connell

Recruiting the Right Kind of People

When it comes to the art of people management and your responsibilities as a people manager, there will always come a time when you will need to hire new team members or new Team Leaders as part of your overall organization. Regardless of whether you are part of a start-up company or part of an already existing and expanding organization, the people you choose to work along side you and your colleagues will need to integrate well into their respective groups and working environments.

The decisions you make on who it is that will be joining your working family will be determined on how prepared you are beforehand and how carefully you have thought out the whole selection process. The same is also true when promoting individuals from within an organization to positions that have become vacant. The over-riding factor for any Manager or Recruitment Officer is their ability to successfully select the candidate that would be of most benefit to their organization while at the same time presenting to the candidates the benefits that such a move would create for them. The word "benefits" in this context should not be exclusive to monitory gains alone but should also take into account the opportunities that exist within a company or organization for further training, development and possible progression. The reasoning behind this is that if you want your business or organization to thrive and be more successful by selecting the best there is, then you will need to offer these people a working environment where they too can thrive. If you don't do this and you only look at the benefits you (the business) will gain from recruiting such personnel then you might as well remain in recruitment mode for ever because one-sided partnerships rarely work.

The Placing of Appointments in the Media:

As we all know, there are a number of ways of attracting new employees in today's ever growing and sometimes competitive employment market. Appointments or advertisements can be placed from anywhere like the local corner shop to specialist recruitment agencies, local, regional and national newspapers, local, regional and national radio, internet recruitment sites, etc. The list is endless and depending on the size of your business, the type of position on offer and of course the amount you're willing to spend will depend on where you want to advertise and who it is you want to read or hear about your offer of employment.

Before sending off that magical advertisement that will hopefully result in finding the perfect person to fill that all important vacancy in your organization you should carefully think about who it is you want to attract as potential candidates. It is becoming more and more critical for all businesses no matter how small or large they may be that not just a little thought but some clever thinking goes into the creating of the advertisement. Many organizations also take this opportunity for their recruitment advertisement to act in part as a promotional tool to the wider audience, portraying an image of an exciting, expanding and caring company to work for and do business with.

The use of specific logos or graphics associated with your business can also have the desired affect. This is generally known as "Branding" and is more successful for certain multi-national organizations where the logo is instantly recognizable.

The better your business comes across to the intended audience, the likelihood of a much higher response rate from the type of candidates you are actually looking for. It is also a smart move to look at what other companies and recruitment agencies are doing to make their advertisements stand out more than others. This is especially true of the more sophisticated ones who will often have the ability of grabbing your attention by the message being relayed as opposed to the use of cheap or inappropriate background effects.

It is imperative that your workplace doesn't give way to racism or any other anti-diversity ways of thinking and / or doing business. Recruitment advertisements should be distributed in an extensive range of media so that the widest cross-section of society will have access to them. You should ensure that they don't contain implicit or explicit discriminatory messages and be sure to include a note stating that you are an equal opportunity employer. In the interview procedure, ensure that you don't use application forms or tests that ask for culturally specific answers.

The basics of your recruitment ad should include the following;
- A brief description on the type of organization or business that you are.
- Vacancy being offered.
- Location.
- What's on offer to the successful candidate.
- The promotional and / or other incentives on offer to candidates who intend to stay longer than the short term.
- The pre-requisites that you would like the applicants to have; both academic and personal – This is solely in relation to the applicants' ability to do the job.
- Closing dates for applications.
- Details on where to send applications.
- Add note on being an Equal Opportunity Employer.

The decision to advertise actual salary is something that companies and organizations view differently. This sometimes depends on the type of position on offer (entry-level employee or managerial) and whether the respective company or organization would be prepared to go beyond what they originally perceived to be fair payment in order to secure a particular type of candidate.

Once you have submitted your masterpiece for publication or airing it is then a good idea to start clarifying with those who will be involved in the interviewing process, the time schedules and methods to be used throughout the interviewing period. Another important point to bear in mind is the setting of a date for the second round of interviews. It is always advisable to re-interview at minimum the top 3 - 5 candidates coming out of the first round. This date needs to be as close to the end of the first round of interviews as possible. Candidates also need to be told at some stage during the first round that this is the method being used and the expected timeframe by which they will know the outcome.

Interviewing Techniques:

Now that an army of prospective candidates are beating a path to your door or so you hope, it is essential that the same positive and creative thinking that went into the recruitment advertisement is now put to use in your interviewing techniques. You really don't want to make the mistake of hiring a sophisticated looking individual with several degrees to their credit only to find out later that they have a number of phobias and suffer from satanic tendencies as it may create a little tension within the workplace.

It makes it much easier if a predetermined list of well thought out questions was drawn up to cover everything from reasons for wanting to leave present job to level of education, previous experience, interpersonal skills, self awareness along with some questions on the persons background and their ambitions for the future. Depending on the country you are in, you will need to be careful that you do not ask questions relating to the individual that are against the law of the land and / or are seen as discriminatory - for example; gender, marital status, religious belief, political opinion, sexual preference / orientation, disability, nationality, race, ethnic origin or age.

It is paramount that the questions being asked are geared in a professional manner to finding out the applicant's ability to do the job as defined in the job spec and not on whether they may be unsuitable due to being male / female / married / handicapped / not from the locality etc.

Your questionnaire should be designed in such a way that it searches for the candidate's level of general intellect (level of education, communication skills etc), emotional intellect (empathy, self awareness including understanding of their own limits and strengths etc) as well as their previous experience and future expectations. The combination of all of these traits coming together will help you in the making of a much more informed and effective decision as to who you believe will be the perfect candidate to fill that all important vacancy. The ideal candidate being someone who comes close to, if not matches, your views on what the "perfect employee", "perfect team leader" or "perfect manager" should be. All going according to plan the chosen candidate should turn out to be a level headed, smart, proactive and effective individual as well as being someone who is a positive contributor to the overall team. Choosing the perfect applicant to suit the position on offer is never easy but with proper preparation it will take you 90% of the way.

A decision will also have to be made as to whether there will only be one interviewer or a panel of interviewers (2 - 3) attending each session. Some organizations feel it is more beneficial to have a pre-arranged panel doing the interviewing as the scores from each candidate have to be averaged to take into account the variances of acceptability by each of the interviewers. It also helps in rare cases where a candidate may feel discriminated against during an interview and where the follow-up investigation relies heavily on testimony from all the interviewers along with the plaintiff in understanding what actually took place.

It's always important that before an interview begins that the interviewer introduces him or her self and talks a little about the company in general and their role in it. A neutral comment about the weather, something making headlines in the news or an enquiry on whether the applicant had any problems finding their way there, will all help to act as an "ice-breaker" in order to help reduce the pre-interview nerves that even the more seasoned candidates may suffer from.

First impressions can just be as important for the interviewee as they are for the interviewer. This is why it's a good idea to remember that if the applicant who has just turned up for the interview is put off by the regimental or unfeeling manner of the interviewer, the company could potentially be loosing the best employee imaginable.

Tools for the Job:

One of the items on an interviewer's check-list that is often overlooked is the type and quality of the interviewing room. It can be very demeaning and distracting for an interviewee to walk into a room that looks more like a storage area with bundles of paper on tables and boxes on the floor. Don't spoil all the good work that has been done up to now by falling into this trap. Make it your business to book an airy and comfortable room with minimalist surroundings so that everyone can concentrate on the actual interview and to do so without any interruptions such as outside noise.

The following is an example of an interview questionnaire that is designed to help in the interviewing of applicants for the role of Team Leader in a manufacturing environment. The questions being asked are designed to help the interviewer better understand the candidates level of education, experience, communication skills, self awareness, ambition and whether the candidate has the attributes of someone who can empathise, be part of, support and motivate those that they work with. This example can be used or modified in any way to suit your own requirements depending on the business you are in and the position being offered.

<u>Interview Questionnaire</u>

Team Leader (Manufacturing)

Name of applicant:

Name of interviewer:

Name of interviewer:

Name of interviewer:

Date: Time:

Notes for Interviewer:

    Answers to the following questions are to be rated 1(poor) – 5(excellent) depending on the accuracy, reasoning, style and fluency of each answer as perceived by you, the interviewer. Contradictions in answers to questions or topics of a similar nature should be noted and further reasoning sought from the interviewee.

    Remember that you are looking for someone that has the desired balance between level of education, experience, communication skills, self awareness, ambition and the attributes of someone who can empathise, be part of, support and motivate those that they work with.

    Overall score to be calculated as per instructions at end of questionnaire.

	Rating:	1	2	3	4	5
Q1 <u>Observation</u> -- Is the candidate presentable? (Appropriately dressed/ groomed)						
Q2 Explain to me what you do on a day-to-day basis within your present job/position?						
Q3 Why are you looking to move from your current role and what is it that attracts you to the role that you are now applying for?						
Q4 What's your absenteeism & timekeeping been like over the past few years?						
Q5 Are you currently on or have you recently been on any disciplinary warnings?						
Q6 How would you use your role as a Team Leader in achieving hourly, daily and weekly targets in productivity, quality and safety?						
Q7 Have you had any experience of LEAN manufacturing (Reducing Waste and Costs) or other related projects?						
Q8 Have you done any Six Sigma (Improving Quality / Reducing Loss) work? Are you certified?						
Q9 What functional (useful, efficient) skills do you have that stand out and would benefit you in the role that you are applying for?						

Q10 What is your current level of education?					
Q11 Have you had any previous experience in the role that you are applying for?					
Q12 Why do you think you deserve this role / position?					
Q13 How committed would you be to all of the overtime requirements?					
Q14 How would you deal with a team of people where absenteeism is seen to be a growing concern?					
Q15 Give me your thoughts on Health & Safety audits and Process audits?					
Q16 How would you go about building an effective team?					
Q17 How would you deal with conflict between two individuals within your group?					
Q18 Give me an example of problem solving? (one process / one people related)					
Q19 Give me an example of priority setting?					
Q20 How would you deal with a situation where your Manager has asked you to do something that you believe would have a negative impact on the process and / or the people concerned?					

Q21 Have you played any part in Health and Safety in the past -- directly or indirectly?					
Q22 What is your current career ambition?					
Q23 How good are you at and how often do you use the following? WORD, EXCEL, POWERPOINT, E-MAIL, INTERNET.					
Q24 What people qualities do you have that would benefit you as a Team Leader?					
Q25 Give me 3 words that best describes you as a person?					
Q26 What are your strengths when dealing with people?					
Q27 What are your weaknesses when dealing with people?					
Q28 How would you deal with a situation where someone else was taking credit for the work that you were doing?					
Q29 How would you go about motivating a group of people that were getting "bogged down" in trying to finish a project on time?					
Q30 How would you recognize signs of stress in both yourself and others?					

Q31 How would you deal with a situation where someone in your team is showing signs of stress and may or may not be under performing of late?					
Q32 Would you consider yourself to be stronger as an individual performer or as a team performer and why?					
Q33 What in your opinion are the positives and negatives in having a multi-cultural workforce?					
Q34 Do you allow "gut feeling" to influence some of your decisions?					
Q35 How would you describe your temperament when dealing with people who show little interest in a job that is of utmost importance?					
Q 36 What is your opinion on the type of questions being asked in this interview?					

Details on overall scoring:

(i) Add the points scored from each of the above questions for an overall score.

(A maximum of 5 points per question multiplied by 36 questions equals a maximum possible score of 180 points)

Overall Score =

(ii) If more than one interviewer was present, calculate the overall average score and note that average as being the final score.

(e.g. 120 + 135 + 115 = 370.   370 divided by 3 = overall average score of 123)

Overall Average Score =

Additional Comments:

_____

_____

_____

When the first round of interviews is coming to a close it should be more than obvious who the top candidates are, going solely on the strength of their interview scores. This kind of approach to the interviewing and selecting of candidates will always come across as an impartial, transparent and professional process. It is always considered prudent to keep all associated documentation in a safe and secure place for at least 12 months, just in case someone (candidate or company) may feel the need to query how the interview was conducted. A fair and impartial interviewing process will always serve you well and it's always nice to have the proof at hand, if required.

Now that you have that small but all important list of top candidates that you would like to see go through to the second round, the following needs to take place as soon as possible.

- Contact each of the successful candidates and confirm that they are still interested in going through to the second round interview – if someone on the list of top candidates has changed their mind for whatever reason, then use your discretion as to whether or not you want to include the individual who had just missed out on the list of top candidates previous to that.

- Once the top list of successful candidates is dealt with then it is important to contact all unsuccessful candidates immediately. This is something that a lot of companies and organizations fail to do with any sense of urgency and as a result, looks unprofessional. Contacting unsuccessful candidates is important from everyone's perspective because it allows those who were unsuccessful on this occasion to continue seeking employment elsewhere and not waste everyone's precious time phoning and writing trying to find out where they stand.
- Repeat when second round of interviews are over.

References / Security checks:

It's important that before the second round of interviews take place that someone has already started to double-check references no matter how well the candidates may have come across during the first round of interviews. It's also just as important to seek assurances on a candidate's past, and this can be done by making contact with the local police and / or any other professional agency that can carry out security checks on a person's background. After all, you don't want to be awake at night thinking about the "Dr. Jekyll and Mr. Hyde" that you may have just hired.

The following examples are only a drop in the ocean as to why a company or organization should always make it their business to perform background checks on prospective candidates entering the final round of interviews; (a) An individual who secured a well paid job with company car and full expenses after supplying details of a University Degree and PhD that they never studied for or received – Yes, it's true and the company only found out long after the event. (b) An individual who secured a job as a customer care representative which involved calling to peoples homes, after supplying false details regarding previous experience – Yes, it's true but fortunately for the company involved, they found out within a few days through an agency that specialises in personnel background checks that this individual had a list of convictions for theft and break-ins. (c) An individual who secured a job in a manufacturing company after supplying stolen I.D. cards as proof of identity – again it is true but luckily for the company involved the police were already keeping tabs on this individual and arrived to arrest him a few days later.

It will often be the case that prospective candidates will present details on previous work experience to his or her prospective employer that may be perceived to be slightly massaged in order to help market themselves in a better light for the position on offer. To most companies and interviewers this is acceptable behaviour and most will argue that it shows intuitive creativity on the part of the interviewee due to the thought process that went into promoting themselves in such a way. It can also be argued however, that the line between intuitive creativity and falsification can sometimes be a tricky one to determine depending on the perspective of the interviewer. I think for most interviewers, especially those with a little interviewing experience under their belt, it should be easy enough to work out the difference between a well presented Resume or Curriculum Vita and what is obviously a list of falsehoods. Then again there is only one way to find out!

Choosing the Right Candidate:

The second round of interviews are often a double checking exercise, going over some of the answers and comments that were given at the first round and possible developing on these as part of a general conversation. It is also the case that a strengthening of relationships will happen at this point between the candidates and the interviewers. Whether it is intentional or not, this relationship building exercise may prove to be more decisive than one might realise.

Imagine a scenario where interviews are over, reference and security checks are in the clear and there are two candidates out of the five that went into the second round now leading the field. Both candidates seem to be outstanding and overall interview scores are very similar. So, the question is, how do you choose? The answer may very well be down to what is known in the emotional intelligence world as "gut feeling" and how well you as an interviewer along with the rest of the panel were able to build a relationship with each of the candidates during the interviewing stage. It is also this ability by one of the candidates to be able to "bond" better with the interviewers that will result in him or her being a preference over the other candidate. Whatever your final decision, it is highly unlikely that you will be disappointed. The thought and preparations that have gone into the interviewing process will have served you well and there is no doubt that your final choice of candidate will be the right person for the job.

Everyday Tips:
- Proper preparation at the advertising stage is critical.
  (If you don't attract the right kind of candidate you won't hire the right kind of candidate)

- Have a tidy and airy room booked in advance for interviewing sessions.
  (The more minimalist the room the higher the possibility of both interviewer and interviewee being able to concentrate fully on the actual interview)

- Be prepared, have your paperwork to hand, act professional and be approachable.
  (The way you come across is how the candidate will see the company)

- Remember that your ideal candidate will be someone with the desired balance between level of education, experience, communication skills, self awareness and ambition as well as being someone who can empathise, be part of, support and motivate those that they work with.

(You will need to be aware of, and receptive to, all of the above in order to be able choose the best possible candidate for the position being offered)

- Give feedback to unsuccessful candidates as soon as possible.

  (Most feedback will be in the form of a "regret letter" but the sooner you do this the sooner the unsuccessful candidates can go looking for employment elsewhere and not waste their time and your time phoning you, looking for an update.

Health & Safety in the Workplace

Already, I can hear you asking why I've included Health & Safety (H & S) in the workplace when this is supposed to be a book that looks in general at people management & people development in the 21st century. Well, the answer is simple. Looking after ourselves and those in our care automatically sends out the message that we have some level of self respect along with empathy and understanding for the welfare of others around us. This can be hugely rewarding in gaining peoples trust and respect especially when you are seen to acknowledge and promote H & S awareness.

Being a leader is all about developing trust between you and your people and there is no better way to form that trust than when your people know they are safe, both physically and metaphorically speaking. It has happened all too often in the past where managers and business owners from all walks of life have gone to the trouble of working out in their heads the type of person they would like to employ next. They then spend time writing out a recruitment ad for the local newspaper or radio, spend time interviewing and selecting that much sought after individual only for the new recruit to injure themselves within a relatively short time of starting work.

Who is affected?

Everyone who enters a place of business is at risk of being in an accident or suffering a set-back in their health, no matter how minute the possibilities may seem. The best purpose-built workplaces in the world with H & S being at the forefront of their planning, regularly encounter H & S issues of some sort. Health and Safety in the workplace is not just about the obvious such as knowing what to do after a severe accident or major incident but should also encompass regular information and training meetings in how to react to a wide variety of situations and most importantly, knowing who to contact when you are unable to successfully deal with a particular situation yourself. The single most important factor for most incidents and accidents is response time and how soon the right kind of help can be sought.

When trying to work out the number of people that may be affected in any given incident or accident it is always best to multiply your answer several fold. The reason for this is because we sometimes only think about those directly evolved in such incidents and accidents and not about the knock-on affect it may have on their closest work colleagues, friends, and of course family. Health and Safety Officers and Managers who do what they can to examine the true impact that any given incident or accident may have, are more likely to be the ones to best educate and inform their workforce of H & S issues in general. This in turn should help greatly in ensuring that their respective working environments are much safer places to be in.

The importance of Self Monitoring:

We should not only look at H & S in the workplace as a law we have to comply with but also as something we need to do for ourselves and those around us. It's important to continuously monitor and improve the layout of our working areas in order to protect everyone that works within that environment. If you are seen by your employees to approach H & S from this angle, not only will you gain their respect but it has been proven time and time again that employees working with this kind of methodology will automatically keep H & S in mind and will endeavour to look after their own areas.

It is also important that supervisors and managers carry out random H & S audits within their respective areas and are seen by their employees to do so. Frequency of audits will depend on potential for injury in the area that you are monitoring. You may need to start with an audit a day or if you feel comfortable that the area in question is relatively safe and all procedures adhered to, it might allow you enough tolerance to carry out a random weekly audit instead.

If the unthinkable ever happens, where there is a serious accident or incident, or worse, then ensure that the area affected is safe before anyone else starts working there again and all requirements of the law of the land are followed through with regard to the proper recording and reporting of accidents or incidents. Hopefully this will never happen to you but in order to reduce the possibilities of a serious incident taking place, H & S has to be approached with a positive frame of mind by all concerned. Always remember, prevention is better than cure.

The type of audit that is drawn up will certainly depend on the business you are in and whether you need to have "Slippery floor" (Hotel / Coffee shop), "Protruding nails" (Building site), "Dangerous equipment" (Manufacturing / Garage) etc. on the list of items to watch out for. Always remember that the best audits are those that are adjusted to take into account the working conditions and potential hazards of the environments that they are meant for and should where possible be carried out on a random basis. This will help to avoid any pre-audit urges by employees to prepare the area just for the sake of the audit. I myself have worked for organizations where there was a "special effort" made by employees, for example on Thursday mornings to ensure that everything was in place for the 11am audit - see what I mean!

Random audits are the only way of coming close to obtaining a true picture of what is really happening. This in turn will help to create a more realistic result regardless of the 96% / 98% /100% overall target you may be aspiring to.

All of this effort will be of little use to anyone if potential hazards that have been found are not rectified a.s.a.p. and a re-audit done shortly afterwards to confirm that the respective area is safe to work in again. If this is not done your credibility will be severely tested.

As well as the list of items to look out for, audits should contain details on the specific area being audited, date & time carried out, itemised & overall pass rate, questions to determine employee awareness of H & S, room for comments and finally supervisory or managerial sign off. It is also important that over time you add any potential hazards you may come across to the overall list of items to look out for in the future.

Tools for the Job:

For all aspects of Health and Safety in the workplace, the following web sites are a wonderful source of information. Not alone are they updated on a regular basis to account for any changes in law but also offer general guidance and advice to both employees and business owners alike.

- European Agency for Safety and Health at Work
  http://europe.osha.eu.int

- Health & Safety Authority Ireland
  / www.hsa.ie

- Health & Safety Executive UK
  www.hse.gov.uk

- Canadian Centre for Occupational Health and Safety
  www.ccohs.ca

- Occupational Safety & Health Administration USA
  www.osha.gov

- Occupational Safety and Health Service New Zealand
  www.osh.dol.govt.nz

- National Occupational Health and Safety Commission
  Australia
  www.nohsc.gov.au

The following is an example of a Job Risk-Assessment Checklist. This will help greatly in the highlighting of potential hazards and causes of injury whether directly or indirectly relating to the processes involved and / or the employee's ability or level of fitness to perform each task successfully.

The Job Risk-Assessment Checklist is usually used for the gathering and evaluating of specific types of information, especially the unknowns in newly created jobs or tasks and even sometimes where processes, circumstances or people in an already evaluated job have changed. The Job Risk-Assessment Checklist is different to a general H & S Audit in that the results will determine the regulations and guidelines to be used before a job can start. The H & S Audit will then monitor an individual's or department's adherence to those regulations and guidelines. This example can be used or modified in any way to suit your own requirements depending on the business you are in and the area being evaluated.

Job Risk-Assessment Checklist

Date: Time:

Auditor:

Job / Task being assessed:

Supervisor / Manager in charge:

***Answers and comments to each of the following questions are to be noted and the job or task being assessed not allowed to proceed unless safe to do.

Process Checklist

- Who is in charge of the job?
- Do their responsibilities overlap with those of anyone else?
- Is there anything which is not someone's responsibility?
- Are there any established safe ways of doing the job?
- Are there any relevant codes of practice or guidance notes?
- Are there safe working procedures laid down for the job?
- Can the job be made safe so that protective clothing is not required?
- Have people been instructed in the use and limitations of protective clothing?

- Has anyone assessed whether equipment, tools or machines have the capacity for the job?
- What will be the consequences if you are wrong?
- How will the person in charge deal with any problems?
- If things do go wrong, would your people know what to do?
- Could emergency services get to the site?
- If the job cannot be finished today, can it be left in a safe state? Are clear instructions available for the next shift?
- Are your production people aware of what the maintenance staff is doing and vice-versa?
- Is there a system for checking that jobs are done safely in the way that they were intended?

People Checklist

- Are the needs or circumstances of the individuals doing the job taken into account?
- People come in all shapes and sizes with different capabilities and levels of fitness. Is there any cause for concern here?
- Protective clothing / gear, type of seating, working space and machinery guarding which are suitable for each individual. Is there any cause for concern here?
- Ability to work safely if they are affected by medication, drugs or alcohol, or have recently suffered illness or injury. Is there any cause for concern here?
- Ability to understand safety instructions, through difference of language or culture. Is there any cause for concern here?
- Appropriate methods, facilities or emergency procedures for those who have partial sight, poor

hearing or some other impairment e.g. epilepsy. Is there any cause for concern here?

Is it safe to continue?   YES   or   NO

Overall Comments:

_____

_____

_____

_____

Signed: H & S Rep or Auditor:

Signed: Supervisor / Manager:

The following are three examples of Health & Safety Audits (Office Area / Canteen Area / Manufacturing Area) that can be used for self monitoring purposes. The layout of the audits are the same but the questions being asked in all three are very different and it is precisely this that makes them effective auditing tools as they focus in on what is relevant for the area they were drawn up for.

This type of self monitoring will in turn help to create a more positive and safer working environment for everyone concerned. These examples can be used or modified in any way to suit your own requirements depending on the business you are in and the area being audited.

Office / Hallway Health & Safety Audit

Date: Time:

Auditor:

Office / Hallway 1st Floor

Pass: Yes/No

1. Are fire exits free of obstructions?	YES	NO
2. Are aisle ways free of obstructions (Boxes etc)?	YES	NO
3. Is there unrestricted access from all areas?	YES	NO
4. Are fire extinguishers unobstructed and seals / pins intact?	YES	NO
5. Are the emergency break-glass units unobstructed?	YES	NO
6. Are all electrical cables etc. free of damage? (Check for damaged and trailing cables)	YES	NO
7. Are all personnel wearing authorised ID Badges?	YES	NO
8. Is there a clear process in place for all tasks?	YES	NO
9. Are work areas free of excessive build up of boxes?	YES	NO
10. Are all chairs free from damage?	YES	NO
11. Are filing cabinets free from being over stacked with files and / or boxes etc?	YES	NO

12. Are filing cabinet doors left in the closed position?	YES	NO
13. Are trash bins being emptied before over spilling occurs?	YES	NO
14. Are office staff ensuring that tea and coffee cup lids are securely in place in order to avoid accidental burns?	YES	NO
15. Is the carpet / tile area free from damage and not a potential trip hazard?	YES	NO

<u>Overall % Pass Rate</u> = Number of items Passed

Divided by number of items on list and multiply by 100

Pass Rate =

Notes on other potential hazards found:

(To be added to above list before next audit)

_____

_____

_____

Employee Awareness

(i) Ask any three employees at random any three of the following questions.

(ii) Incorrect answers to be highlighted by placing an X in the box after the question.

(iii) Place a tick after each employee's name who answered all questions correctly.

Maurice O'Connell

Employee name: _____

_____

Employee name: _____

_____

Employee name: _____

_____

1. Where is the nearest fire extinguisher located?	
2. Where is the nearest fire exit located?	
3. Who is the Area Safety Representative?	
4. Who is the First-Aid person for this area?	
5. What is the emergency evacuation procedure?	
6. Who is allowed to give the all clear following an evacuation?	

Supervisor / Manager Sign-off

Office / Hallway 1st Floor: _____

_____

Additional Comments:

_____

_____

Canteen / Kitchen Health & Safety Audit

Date: Time:

Auditor:

Canteen / Kitchen

	Pass:	Yes/No
1. Is the floor area free from spillages and if spillages are present, are appropriate signs in place and have staff been notified?	YES	NO
2. Is there an adequate walkway between each row of tables?	YES	NO
3. Are all tables clear of rubbish and unused tables immediately cleaned?	YES	NO
4. Are the locations of the Fire Extinguishers clearly marked and seals / pins intact?	YES	NO
5. Are all staff who are involved in food preparation and serving, wearing appropriate gloves / hair-nets / hats?	YES	NO
6. Are aisle-ways and floors free of debris and refuse, allowing unobstructed access to the Fire Exits?	YES	NO
7. Are the Fire Exits unobstructed (including the exit in the kitchen?)	YES	NO

8. Are the Bain-Marie's fitted with lids to prevent steam burns?	YES	NO
9. Are the Carousels working correctly?	YES	NO
10. Are the floor mats near the exit to the Smoking Area sitting properly on the floor and not a potential trip hazard?	YES	NO
11. Are the tray trolleys stored correctly?	YES	NO
12. Are all serving areas / surfaces wiped clean?	YES	NO
13. Are all cleaning materials stored in the designated area when not in use?	YES	NO
14. Is the cleaning schedule for the freezers being adhered to?	YES	NO
15. Are refrigeration units maintaining recommended temperatures and is this being monitored frequently?	YES	NO
16. Are meat products being stored correctly? (Raw / Cooked meats stored separately to prevent cross - contamination)	YES	NO
17. Are hoods fitted to deep fat fryers when they are not in use?	YES	NO
18. Are all staff members wearing correct safety clothing?	YES	NO

Overall % Pass Rate = Number of items Passed

Divided by number of items on list and multiply by 100

Pass Rate =

Notes on other potential hazards found:
(To be added to above list before next audit)

_____

_____

_____

Employee Awareness

(i) Ask any three employees at random any three of the following questions.

(ii) Incorrect answers to be highlighted by placing an X in the box after the question.

(iii) Place a tick after each employee's name who answered all questions correctly.

Employee name: _____

_____

Employee name: _____

_____

Employee name: _____

_____

1. Where is the nearest fire extinguisher located?	
2. Where is the nearest Fire Exit located?	
3. Who is the Area Safety Representative?	
4. Who is the First-Aid person for this area?	
5. What is the emergency evacuation procedure?	
6. Who is allowed to give the all clear following an evacuation?	

Supervisor / Manager Sign-off

Canteen / Kitchen area: _____

_____

Additional Comments:

_____

_____

_____

Manufacturing Area Health & Safety Audit

Date: Time:

Auditor:

Manufacturing Area 01

Pass: Yes/No

1. Boxes on pallets are stacked to a reasonable height? (approx. 1.5 metres high)	YES	NO
2. Empty Pallets are stored correctly on designated checker plates?	YES	NO
3. Aisle-ways are free of debris and allow adequate access to emergency exits?	YES	NO
4. Trolleys are stored in the correct locations and there are no excess trolleys?	YES	NO
5. Fire extinguishers are not blocked and all pins / seals intact?	YES	NO
6. Personnel are using the correct tools? (Safety Knives / Tape Guns / Safety Screw Drivers etc)	YES	NO
7. Relevant personnel are wearing appropriate Safety Clothing / Gear? (Footwear / Hi Visibility Vests / Ear Muffs as per notices in each area)	YES	NO
8. Personnel are using correct Manual-handling techniques?	YES	NO
9. The Trash Conveyor is not overloaded? (adequate time is allowed for trash to clear)	YES	NO

10. Operators are not stacking trash around them?	YES	NO
11. Fatigue Matting is in good condition and correctly secured?	YES	NO
12. All mechanically operated items have safety gates that are functioning correctly and are being used correctly?	YES	NO
13. Personnel using machinery are trained and licensed where necessary?	YES	NO
14. Where mechanical hoists are provided, they are being used correctly?	YES	NO
15. Personnel are not wearing headphones? (radio / media player)	YES	NO

Overall % Pass Rate = Number of items Passed

Divided by number of items on list and multiply by 100

Pass Rate =

Notes on other potential hazards found:

(To be added to above list before next audit)

_____

_____

_____

_____

Employee Awareness

(i) Ask any three employees at random any three of the following questions.

(ii) Incorrect answers to be highlighted by placing an X in the box after the question.

(iii) Place a tick after each employee's name who answered all questions correctly.

Employee name: _____

_____

Employee name: _____

_____

Employee name: _____

_____

1. Where is the nearest fire extinguisher located?	
2. Where is the nearest Fire Exit located?	
3. Who is the Area Safety Representative?	
4. Who is the First-Aid person for this area?	
5. What is the emergency evacuation procedure?	
6. Who is allowed to give the all clear following an evacuation?	

Supervisor / Manager Sign-off

Area 01: _____

Additional Comments:

_____

_____

Everyday Tips:

- Highlight or question anything that could potentially result in an injury or incident.
  (Responsiveness from the top helps to heighten the awareness of others)

- Accompany the H & S Rep or Auditor as often as possible during auditing time.
  (Your presence during auditing will portray importance of H & S to those watching)

- Help to put closure to any potential hazards or other H & S issues a.s.a.p.
  (Your credibility will be severely tested if this does not happen)

- Regularly ask people about their well being – Have they any concerns?
  (Being approachable can often uncover potential hazards sooner rather than later. Showing a personal interest will also help you in getting to know your people)

- Remember that a healthy and safe working environment is reassuring for all.

  (Reduced absenteeism and associated costs for all parties concerned. Guaranteed increase in productivity due to everyone being at work. Increased morale amongst employees due to safety of working environment)

People Management

People management is all about getting your people and teams to do what you need them to, in order to run a successful business. The role of the Team Leader, Supervisor, Manager or Director as the pinnacle of their respective teams is to be able to communicate effectively with all those around them including their subordinates, peers and superiors. This is absolutely critical in the successful running of any day-to-day business.

Effective Communication:

The difference between effective and non-effective communication in the workplace is the equivalent to one group knowing exactly what needs to be done and how to do it compared to another group who are pulling in all directions due to the various interpretations of what they believe was said or asked of them. It is also critical to the future success of any business that the employees genuinely feel that they are a valued part of what is taking place and that the supervisors and managers are fully tuned into this way of thinking. This is why effective communication by management to their employees has to include a genuine acknowledgment that the employees are the ones that make it all happen and words to that affect need to be said and said often.

It is vital however; that continuous constructive feedback takes place between the Team Leader and his/her subordinates. This, for the most part, will be informal get-togethers around the working environment but at the same time needs to be honest and effective without being unnecessarily extreme. The difference between continuous constructive criticism with well-balanced feedback and continuous negative feedback in the name of constructive criticism is that the former will leave most people with a sense of empowerment and the ability to achieve their targets while the latter will almost certainly leave people feeling dejected and with an increasing sense of inability of ever meeting their targets regardless of what they do. Make sure you know the difference between the two.

A breakdown of communication within a team or between teams can lead to mistrust, conflict, stress and loss of morale amongst the individuals caught up in the everyday frustrations of trying to do what they believe is best. A good Team Leader, Supervisor or Manager will ensure that their people fully understand what is expected of them while at the same time being receptive to their needs and concerns. It is a win-win situation for everyone concerned when the Team Leader, Supervisor or Manager has the ability to give direction as per the needs of the business while at the same time being able chat to people on a more personal level. Knowing your people and being able to communicate effectively with them will lead to a long term positive partnership.

The Rippling Affect:

Regardless of who we are in life it is important to bear in mind that our actions, both positive and negative can have a direct and indirect knock-on effect on others around us. This is similar to someone throwing a pebble into a pool of water and watching the ripples travel outwards from the point of contact, disturbing the calm surface as they continue in a determined and unstoppable mode. That is why we call the result of our actions on others - The Rippling Affect. As a Team Leader, Supervisor or Manager it is important to continuously monitor the actions and behavioural patterns of individuals within your team. This will help you in pin-pointing those who are having a positive or negative impact on the immediate team as well as the knock-on effect it may be having on other groups that you interact with and rely on, in order to get business done. A good Team Leader, Supervisor or Manager won't spend their time solely looking for negative actions and behavioural patterns but will just be as eager in seeking out the positives in people and highlighting and promoting these in a way that it becomes acknowledged as best practice.

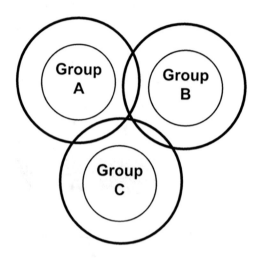

Looking at the above diagram, imagine that you are the Manager of Group C. You have a couple of individuals who are not the easiest of people to get on with and are also a little disruptive when working with other team members. The rippling affect from these individuals on others around them is going to be a negative one and will have an adverse effect on the team as a whole. This may result in some members feeling uncomfortable about working in such an environment which in turn may lead to stress and even absenteeism. It is also true that members from Groups A & B will be very wary of who they interact with from Group C and may avoid the group altogether unless absolutely necessary to do so.

If it comes to a point where other team members, or worse still, other groups are starting to make complaints then a certain amount of damage has already been done to interdepartmental relations. This can make it very difficult for you as a Team Leader, Supervisor or Manager to re-kindle the level of confidence that has been lost within your own group and with those from other groups that you need to interact with.

Note: As a Team Leader, it is imperative that you put a stop to all kinds of negativity developing within your group, sooner rather than later, in order to put a stop to the negative rippling affect it may be having on others.

Now let's imagine that you are the Manager of Group A and you are fortunate enough to have several individuals within your team who have a strong positive attitude towards their work and are always willing to help others around them. The rippling affect from these individuals is going to be a very positive one, helping to elevate even further the positive attitudes of others within the team. This will also create a less stressful working environment and will result in your group being a far more productive one. There is also a strong possibility that members from Groups B & C will find members of Group A very easy to do business with and will automatically interact with them whenever they can. The reason for this is that the positive rippling affect emanating from Group A is now having a positive effect on Groups B & C, which is also making it easier on them when getting their work done.

Note: As a Team Leader, praising your team for work well done and how they are being positively viewed by others will help greatly in the enhancing of working relations and the feeling of euphoria that may already exist within your group.

At this stage you are probably wondering about the Manager in Group B. This time we are going to look at Group B from a different angle. I want you to imagine that you are an outsider looking in on the overall group. Within this group there is a particular team member (Shane) who needs to liaise with members of Groups A & C in order to get his own work done successfully. Not alone is he having problems proceeding with his own work due to issues in Group C but Group A are also unable to keep to their schedule which again is due to issues within Group C. The negative rippling affect from Group C is now having a serious impact on several departments and a lot of people are starting to feel the pressure.

Shane is starting to suffer as a result of someone else's inability or unwillingness to do their job correctly and immediately informs his Supervisor (Miranda) of what is happening. As part of the meeting it is discussed where the problem is originating from and the impact it is having on Shane as well as others. Shane is adamant however that he doesn't want his name used as the one who informed on the other group. Miranda empathises with Shane on the difficulties he is having to face in getting the job done and promises to deal with it immediately. As promised, Miranda first talks to her counterpart in Group A to gather more evidence and together they meet with the next level Manager to inform him of what is happening. She then meets with Shane again, just to let him know that the situation is being dealt with and without any reference to him. Within a couple of days Shane starts to see an improvement in the quality of work arriving into him and a positive shift towards overall working relations.

Note: As a Team Leader, it is hugely important that your people feel comfortable in being able to approach you on a range of matters and that you can act as confidant when asked to do so. To have peoples trust will help greatly in the strengthening of relations between you and members of your team which in turn will reap its own rewards during the bad times as well as the good.

It is in rare cases like this that a Team Leader from one particular group may have to initiate a move in order to put a stop to the negative rippling affect from other departments. Even though the rippling affect from Group C was negative, Miranda's move to put a stop to it was creating a more powerful and positive rippling affect. This in turn won the day and generally speaking, has to, in order for business to survive.

Tools for the Job:

There is a lot to be said for Team Leaders who can talk to their people in a relaxed and trusting manner and to be able to build a good working relationship on that basis. Every now and again however, it will be necessary to have a formal One-to-One meeting with your subordinates such as the end-of-quarter or end-of-year reviews. There may also be other times during the year when a Team Leader, Supervisor or Manager might feel that a One-to-One is warranted, be it for positive or negative reasons.

One of the most effective ways of having a formal One-to-One meeting is through a carefully pre-designed document that has a few well chosen, open-ended questions that are written in such a way that it initiates a two way conversation. This is absolutely essential in order to allow the employee and the Team Leader / Supervisor / Manager to have a meaningful and effective One-to-One meeting with regards to all aspects of their work.

One-to-One

General

Employee:

Supervisor / Manager:

Date:

This One-to-One is an opportunity for the employee and the Supervisor / Manager to have an honest and opened minded discussion regarding all aspects of their work. The meeting should include discussions on the working environment and working relations. This One-to-One should also be used as an opportunity to first discuss and then to note any actions for improvement.

1. Are there any issues or topics that the employee would like to discuss and / or have noted as part of this meeting. (Good / Bad – Positive / Negative)

Note: Can revert back to this question at any time.

(a)_____

_____

(b)_____

_____

(c)_____

_____

(d)_____

_____

2. Issues or topics that the Supervisor / Manager would like to discuss

(a) Concerns or issues if any:

_____

_____

_____

(b) Positives - What has gone well:

_____

_____

_____

(c) Observations / Coaching – Ideas for improvement:

_____

_____

_____

3. Is there anything else that I as your Supervisor / Manager can do to help make your Job easier?

_____

_____

_____

_____

_____

Follow up actions:

(i) What actions are being taken from this meeting?

(ii) Who is taking responsibility for each action? (Employee or Supervisor / Manager)

(iii) Agree a due date.

Important: Follow-up actions must be S.M.A.R.T.

(Specific, Measurable, Achievable, Results oriented, Time specific)

Action:	Responsibility	Due Date

We will meet again in approx _____to monitor progress of above actions or sooner if deemed necessary.

Signed Supervisor / Manager:

_____

Signed Employee

_____

No matter how well or smoothly you may think your department is running, there will always be a time when you will need to work out why something is not going according to plan or to "root cause" a specific problem. Depending on the nature of the problem and the size of the organization you are working within, this can sometimes seem like a complex and daunting task especially if there are several people or departments involved.

One of the simplest but most effective tools for investigating or root causing such problems was usually known as "The Five Whys" and typically refers to the practice of asking each affected individual "Why?" something is not going according to plan and to keep asking "Why?" of each individual or department until the root cause of the problem is found. It works on the following principle; when something goes wrong or someone cannot do their job properly, it is usually due to a direct or indirect knock-on effect from something else happening previous to that. Remember the Rippling Affect from earlier?

In the past however, many Managers including myself have found that for all its wonders and its simplicity of use, The Five Whys tool had to be modified in order to maximise it effectiveness, sometimes because we needed to ask the question "why?", more times than just five. It also became essential that more sections were added in order to maximise its potential as a worthy investigative tool and problem solver. The sections I've added here, include; "What is wrong?", "Conclusion", "Suggestions for Improvement", "People who will be sent copies of this Report", "Other Comments" and a signature line for the Investigating Manager.

With these sections now added it has become a far more powerful investigative tool. Not only can it be used to investigate and root-cause almost any problem imaginable but also to report on it and offer suggestions for future improvements which should lead to a permanent resolution. With these modifications in place, I've now re-named it the "Why Investigation" tool.

<u>Why Investigation</u>

Date:

Department / Area where issue has been raised:

Investigating Manager:
What is wrong?

_____

_____

WHY?

_____

_____

WHY?

_____

_____

WHY?

_____

_____

WHY?

_____

_____

WHY?

_____

_____

WHY?

_____

_____

Conclusion:

_____

_____

Suggestions for Improvement:

_____

_____

People who will be sent copies of this Report:

_____

_____

Other Comments:

_____

_____

Singed Investigating Manager:

_____

The following are two actual examples of problems that were resolved using this method. Both examples are as close to actual events that I can remember but without compromising the names of the people or the organizations involved. Both examples given here were investigated by myself and my then superiors and resolved as a result of using the Why Investigation tool. The first example is a little complicated and shows what can happen within a large organization. The second is not as complicated but the positive results from using this tool are just the same. You will also notice that the amount of times you ask the question "why?" will depend on how far you need to go before discovering the root cause.

Example 1:

<u>Why Investigation</u>

Date: XX / XX / XXXX

Department / Area where issue has been raised:
Manufacturing floor – Area 1

Investigating Manager:
Mr. Some Body
What is wrong? ------ Bad quality product being produced from machine.

Operator on manufacturing floor has complained that he is unable to get a consistent flow of quality from the machine he is using.

WHY? ----- Operator.
No matter how many adjustments the operator makes to the machine he cannot get it to work correctly. He estimates that the amount of defective product being thrown away could be worth thousands. He suspects that part of the tooling has worn out and needs replacing. The operator has highlighted the issue to the maintenance crew on several occasions but it seems like nothing is being done.

WHY? ------ Maintenance crew.
Maintenance crew are fully aware of the issue and have tried on several occasions in the past week to order the necessary part from an outside supplier. The supplier is temporarily

refusing to send the part due to an issue they have with the finance department where there is a delay in payment for goods they've already sent us several months ago.

WHY? ------ Finance department.

Finance personal are aware of the outstanding payments due to the outside supplier but have been asked by their Senior Manager to hold off payment for another four days which will take them into the first of next month. This is due to this months budgeting threshold being surpassed and the department being under pressure to tighten up and reduce overall costs.

WHY? ---- Senior Finance Manager.

Senior Finance Manager is aware of a number of overdue payments being held back until the first of next month but is fully prepared to spend on items that are critical to the business and which will ultimately save money. All that has to happen is for the Manufacturing Manager to meet with him or any other Finance Department Supervisor or Manager and explain why urgent action is required. All other finance department Supervisors and Managers are aware of this agreement and can act accordingly in his absence. It is the first that he has heard about this issue and will immediately release payment to the necessary supplier and ask that the required part be sent immediately by express courier.

WHY? ---- Manufacturing Manager.

Manufacturing Manager is fully aware of the issue regarding the defective machine. He is at a loss as to why the Finance

Manager does not know about the issue as he sent an e-mail to one of the girls in the Finance Department three days ago while her Senior Manager was away on business explaining how urgent the situation was and to escalate the matter to her immediate Manager a.s.a.p. He admits that he had not time to chase up on it due to other commitments.

WHY? ---- Finance Department
The girl in question had been out sick for over a week with no one else having access to her e-mail. On opening the respective e-mail it shows that no one else was copied on it. Both the Finance Manager and the girl that the e-mail was sent to only returned to work today.

Conclusion:

There is a lack of proper communication and understanding between all departments. This has become quite evident considering the impact that the faulty machine was having on the people directly involved in trying to keep it operational and those looking for ways of fixing it – not to mention the out-of-control financial losses being incurred. What was also evident was the lack of proper feedback, where some individuals were unaware of the reasons for the hold up which in itself was leading to stress.

Suggestions for improvement:
    (i) All issues needing outside departmental help need to be communicated to both the Supervisor and Manager

of those departments by their respective opposites within the department where the issue is occurring.

(ii) Anyone sending e-mails or other forms of communication regarding a specific issue must copy where possible all those affected as well as those whose help is being asked. If the issue is having a serious impact, for whatever reason, then all communication needs to state this.

(iii) Issues not being resolved must be escalated according to the agreed escalation path and timeframe.

(iv) All Departmental Managers to communicate this to their respective teams' a.s.a.p.

People who will be sent copies of this report:

Managing Director, Senior Managers, Departmental Managers, Departmental Supervisors.

Other Comments:

An audit will be done in the near future to confirm that the above has taken place.

Singed Investigating Manager:
Mr. Some Body

Example 2:

<u>Why Investigation</u>

Date: XX / XX / XXXX

Department / Area where issue has been raised:
Hotel – HR Department

Investigating Manager:
Mrs. Some Body-Else

What is wrong? ------- Two relatively new employees have received each others wages along with a mix-up in personal details.

WHY? ----- H.R. Manager.
HR Manager double-checks personnel records for exact details of what was submitted by each Department Supervisor during the week of hiring. All details match up.

WHY? ------ Department Supervisor.
Department Supervisor remembers going through some paperwork from a number of new recruits before handing them over to H.R. He also admits to accidentally mixing up the paperwork from a number of the new recruits but had thought that everything was rectified before submitting the complete folder to the H.R. Department.

WHY? ----   N/A

WHY? ---- N/A

WHY? ---- N/A

WHY? ---- N/A

Conclusion:

Department Supervisor didn't show enough attention to detail when trying to recover from the accidental mix-up.

Suggestions for improvement:

(i) Department Supervisor needs to be aware of the stress caused to the new recruits and the unprofessional image that has been portrayed as a result of the accidental mix-up.

(ii) Department Supervisor needs to meet with the two girls immediately and apologise for his actions ensuring them that all personal and pay related details will be rectified a.s.a.p.

(iii) Department Supervisor's attention to detail in general may need to be monitored by his immediate Manager.

People who will be sent copies of this report:

Department Supervisor, First level Manager, H.R. Manager

Other Comments:

The two girls must to be involved in ensuring that all details are correct before resubmitting to the H.R. Department for a second time.

Singed Investigating Manager:

Mrs. Some Body-Else

Everyday Tips:

- Always do your best to communicate effectively – Be Credible.

  (Effective communication is all about the credibility of a Manager or organization. Credibility for the Manager or organization means that they regularly communicate with their employees about the company's directions and plans and even asks for ideas on such matters. It involves the co-ordinating of people and resources efficiently and effectively so that employees know how their work relates to the company's goals. To be credible, words must be followed by actions.)

- Be conscious of the Rippling Affect.

  (Whenever we do something in life, be it positive or negative, it will nearly always have an impact on others around us. This is something that all people Managers need to be aware of and the impact that everyone's actions, or lack of, may have on others within and possibly outside of the team. Remember that negative rippling affects need to be sourced, investigated and halted while positive rippling affects need to be better understood and promoted.)

- Have regular One-to-One meetings.
  (One-to-One meetings can be a powerful platform from which any two people can confidently and confidentially discuss their current perceptions regarding their work and the possibilities for maximising their true potential. As the head of your respective group or team, it is important to make the most of this simple but powerful management tool which will help greatly in gaining peoples trust and resulting in a well balanced, proactive and productive team.)

People Development

People development as an ongoing process will mean different things to different Managers and organizations. Some will argue that people management and people development are two separate entities and should always be treated as such while others will argue that the two are very much intertwined and therefore inseparable as they are both necessary in the helping of individuals and teams alike to realise a common goal. I tend to agree with the latter and even more so where people management and people development run close to and parallel with each other. It should be like travelling on a dual-carriageway to the future where you can change lanes as often as necessary, depending on whether it's a management or development mode you are in.

A person should be able to get the training and development they need without it causing too much interference with the everyday running of the business and to be able to slip in and out of what ever mode is required without them feeling like they had to leave the road they were on in the first place. The more experienced you become in both management and development the better you'll be able to decide for yourself which lane it is that you and your team members need to be in at any given time. This parallel way of thinking will help to maximise the benefits you get from training and development in order to avoid the "pot-holes" of the future.

Team Building (Training and Development):

Whatever your philosophy may be on the implementations of training and development and its associations with people management, the only people managers who will really succeed in the future are those with a heightened awareness of themselves and others around them. They will need to be capable of fusing both management and development needs together in such a way that they produce the most effective results possible for everyone concerned.

The benefits of team building can be hugely rewarding for any organization, both from a business and a people perspective. The results of these benefits can usually be divided into two segments, highly visual and sublime, both of which are extremely important. The highly visual segment consisting of benefits like; better productivity, less downtime and less absenteeism. The sublime segment consisting of benefits like; more trust between individuals, a build up of confidence and less stress.

The aim of any team building exercise regardless of whether it is through defined training sessions or the more everyday simplistic approach such as neutral eye contact and the friendly hello, how are you?, is to continuously improve the capabilities and relations between all individuals within the workplace. This in turn will help to create a more pro-active and less stressful working environment while continuing to drive the needs of the overall business.

The big question for anyone with the responsibility for managing and developing a group of people; is where do you start? Trying to decide what kind of training and development is most important and who in your team should be attending first, is not always easy. There needs to be a structured and profound approach to the highlighting of the development needs of both individuals and teams a like. It is crucial that an individual's or team's development needs are properly investigated and understood before being implemented. If this does not happen then the system is prone to creating some very expensive mistakes - not all of which are monetary. It is also very possible to have a structured and profound approach to training and development without getting bogged down in bureaucracy or "red tape".

Let's look at two examples of methods used in trying to decide the appropriate training needs of individuals in a multi-national organization as approached by someone in a foreign office.

Example 1

A large multinational organization is implementing a series of training programs for all of its employees worldwide with a target completion date set for only 4 months away. The training programs to be implemented were chosen by the head of training after he met with various employees and H.R. personnel in his building (Company H.Q.). The meetings were informal One-to-One's and their objective was to get a better understanding of what was actually required. This in turn would help him in sourcing more suitable training material to advance the potential of both the employees and the company as a whole. Once drafted, the training material would be rolled out across all locations.

The first positive thing that stands out here are the One-to-One's that the head of training had with various employees and members of the H.R. Department. This would have given a number of people the opportunity to talk about parts of the programs that they felt were important to them and given them the opportunity to suggest modifications to the programs that might help in how they were implemented or delivered. It would also have given the people involved a sense of importance and made them feel part of this new move forward. The head of training could also adjust and tailor the training material to suit the requirements of the people that he was aiming it at which would make it easier and more acceptable to everyone involved.

Here however, is where all the good work begins to fall apart. There is a very strong possibility that the only people that will truly feel excited and part of this training program will be from within the building where it was discussed and developed. People elsewhere may have different requirements and different cultural elements within their immediate organization that would affect what and how any training material was delivered. It could turn out to be a very costly mistake indeed.

Example 2

A large multinational organization is implementing a series of training programs for all of its employees worldwide with a target completion date set for only 4 months away. The training programs to be implemented were chosen by the head of training after he met with various employees and H.R. personnel in his building (Company H.Q.). The meetings were informal One-to-One's and their objective was to get a better understanding of what was actually required. This in turn would help him in sourcing more suitable training material to advance the potential of both the employees and the company as a whole. Once drafted, the training material would be sent to the Training Managers in offices elsewhere in the world with specific instructions for these Managers to meet with some of their respective employees and H.R. personnel in order to see how each program could be tailored to suit the needs of the people in those regions. Areas to consider when tailoring each program should include but not be limited to; suitability of program within each working environment, cultural differences and law of the land. It is also imperative that the overall message and aim of each training program not be distorted or lost by any of the changes that are deemed necessary.

In this example the views of several Managers, H.R. personnel and employees from various parts of the world are asked for and local elements such as working environments, local culture and law of the land taken into consideration. The same sense of importance that the people in the first example had has now spread throughout the whole company which now gives a lot of people in different regions the feeling that they were partly responsible for creating this new move forward.

So the important lesson here is, no matter how brilliant an idea may be, unless you get a number of people from the wider audience to "buy into" the whole concept, there is always a strong possibility that it will not succeed like it should. Try comparing this to the positive impact your idea might have if others were also helping you to promote it in their own locations, be it a different department or a different part of the world.

Morale Building:

Morale building is often looked upon by many Team Leaders as being an uncertain and tricky area to enter into where the overall aim is to successfully entice your people as individuals and as a group to be more eager and proactive in everything they do regarding their working life. The whole art of morale building is a unique blend of people management and people development where you will need to draw on both your traditional and emotional intellectual abilities. These abilities will need to be cleverly used in conjunction with each other in order to maximise their affect. It is essential that people managers understand the importance of morale building and how it feeds into the whole area of team building and business success.

Being a successful morale builder is much like being a successful doctor whose waiting room is slowly but surely filling as the day progresses. The doctor knows that the waiting room is gradually filling but each patient that enters his or her private room is given their full attention and they will listen to and consult with each patient as if they were the only patient in the world. Whatever ailments the patients may have had or however grumpy they may have felt before going in to see the doctor, it is usually the case that they leave with a new sense of well-being and once again have the desire and the eagerness to meet life head on – sound familiar? The word successful in this context does not mean how fast the doctor can reduce the waiting time for each patient though I'm sure that it is an important part of a doctors remit but what it does mean is the doctors ability to "inject" a new eagerness into his or her patients just by the fact of being able to allow each patient the time to feel that they are the most important person there.

So, the question is how can we successfully translate what takes place in the doctor's private room and implement it as part of the everyday business world and especially to the area of morale building? The answer is not at all as complicated as some might think but it does require the Team Leader, just like the doctor, to be able empathise with the individual they are meeting and be receptive to their needs which will give each individual a sense of importance. A major starting point with regards to morale building is all about listening and being receptive to the individuals needs even if it is not always possible to resolve some of the issues being discussed. The fact that you have given your undivided attention to each individual will in turn give that individual a better sense of belonging, be it for life in general or the place where they work. This in turn will bring out the eagerness and proactive-ness in them to continue to do the best they can.

To be able to listen to what people are saying, even if at times you may have little interest in the actual topic of conversation is a kind of maturity that develops with experience. It is of utmost importance that you show interest and be able to allow the individual the time to convey their thoughts or ideas. People in general who feel that they have someone who cares enough to give them that time, to talk about whatever concerns they may have or whatever it is that makes them happy, are very often the same people who will look upon that person - be it the Doctor, Team Leader, Supervisor, Manager or whoever - as being an important part of their life and they will for the most part do what they can to support them.

As a Manager you will need to use these morale building skills to find out what tools, resources, clearer communications, expectations, rewards and workplace norms need monitoring, improving or implementing in order for your workforce to be more effective, more efficient and more optimistic. Some people within the workforce may be shocked to see that you're willing to listen to both good and bad news and even more surprised when you set out to do something about the suggestions they've made. That initial shock will turn into greater commitment to the job, a renewed interest in working together, more willingness to collaborate and greater permission for individuals in general to be more honest with you as their Team Leader and each other. Again, the simple things like neutral eye contact and the regular hello can often be the "ice-breakers" and the gateway to a better working relationship.

Acknowledging the individuals within your team and acknowledging their efforts towards the company's or organization's overall success is a very positive and proactive form of management, development and morale boosting - all rolled into one.

Tools for the Job:

There are several ways of homing in on the potential for development within your team. Two of the most effective ways of doing this are the One-to-One's, similar to those discussed under People Management and the far more advanced 360-degree feedback program.

The One-to-One document drawn up here is in ways

similar to the one used in People Management, in that it needs to be a carefully thought out document with just a few well chosen, open-ended questions that will initiate a two way conversation. This is absolutely essential in order to allow the employee and the Team Leader, Supervisor or Manager to have a meaningful and effective One-to-One meeting with regards to all aspects of training and development. The questions being asked here should be geared very much towards how employees at all levels feel regarding their present level of training and development. It will also help the interviewer in uncovering their thoughts and concerns surrounding any forthcoming training and development material. This example can be used or modified in any way to suit your own requirements, depending on the business you are in.

One-to-One

Investigating Training and Development needs.

Employee:

Department:

Supervisor / Manager:

Date:

This One-to-One is an opportunity for the employee and the Supervisor / Manager to have an honest and opened minded discussion regarding all aspects of training and development within the employee's department. The meeting should include discussions on present levels of training and development and the positives and negatives of same. This One-to-One should also be used as an opportunity to discuss any forthcoming training and development material and its suitability at this time.

1. Are there any issues concerning the present level of training and development that the employee would like to discuss and / or have noted as part of this meeting? We are genuinely interested in all kinds of feedback; Good / Bad – Positive / Negative.

Note: Can revert back to this question at any time.

(a)_____

_____

(b)_____

_____

(c)_____

_____

(d)_____

_____

2. Issues or concerns regarding training and development that the Supervisor / Manager would like to discuss. This includes results of past training and development and thoughts surrounding any future training and development.

(a) Concerns if any:

_____

_____

(b) Positives - What has gone well / What is planned:

_____

_____

(c) Observations – Mistakes and successes from the past / Ideas for the future:

_____

_____

3. Q. Is there anything else that I as your Supervisor / Manager can do to help maximise your own and your departments training and development?

_____

_____

_____

_____

Follow up actions:

(i) What actions are being taken from this meeting?

(ii) Who is taking responsibility for each action? (Employee or Supervisor / Manager)

(iii) Agree a due date.

Important: Follow up actions must be S.M.A.R.T.

(Specific, Measurable, Achievable, Results oriented, Time specific)

Action:	Responsibility	Due Date

We will meet again in approx _____to discuss progress of above actions or sooner if deemed necessary.

Signed Supervisor / Manager:

_____

Signed Employee

_____

The 360 degree feedback program should only be presented to individuals and groups of people who have been doing a certain job or have been working together for a while. This is necessary in order to allow people to get to know and understand each other.

The effectiveness and success of the 360 degree feedback program really depends on the willingness by everyone to give and receive feedback in a genuine, open minded and honest manner. If a large proportion of your organization is uncomfortable with doing this then it may be best to hold off for a while until they are willing to "buy into" the benefits that can result from such an exercise.

It may be wise to advertise and promote the 360 degree feedback program for a couple of weeks in advance highlighting all the benefits that can result from such an exercise. The 360 degree feedback program is hugely successful because of its unique design in being able to obtain information on individuals as perceived through the eyes of others. A word of caution however; people's honesty in their views of others needs to be taken by the recipients in a mature and open minded fashion. Failure by certain recipients to accept the views of others in the way that they were intended could be highly damaging to their respective groups due to a build-up of tension. If as a Team Leader / Supervisor / Manager you are confident that your group or organization are mature enough to handle the methods used in this kind of information gathering exercise, especially when its sole use is for training and development purposes, then it is highly likely that you will uncover a truer picture of what is actually happening in the workplace and what is genuinely required to improve it.

The question as to anonymity of respondents is up to you. A grown-up organization with grown-up people should be able to cope with, and derive more benefit from, operating the process transparently - but it is a decision that you as a Team Leader will need to take. There will always be a percentage of people who would prefer to give feedback anonymously due to a fear of repercussions when telling the truth just as there will always be a percentage of recipients who will not be able to deal particularly well with criticism from a named individual.

The 360 degree feedback program sees each team member including Team Leaders, Supervisors and Managers performing a self-assessment before being assessed by his or her peers, superiors and subordinates. This enables individuals to review their own strengths and weaknesses as a result of how they are perceived by others against how they see themselves. The reason for this; is that we don't always see ourselves in the same way or as clearly as others might see us. In order to get a reasonably picture of what you and your team are really like it is important that everyone who participates in this exercise are as honest and genuine as they can be with their own as well as everyone else's assessment.

It is important that your team members like and respect each other. If the feedback has revealed such serious conflicts between some individuals in the team that they cannot be rectified then you may have no other choice but to separate them. This extremity in the workplace is rare mainly because it takes a good mix of personalities within each group to help make the working environment an interesting place to be in. Having nothing but introverts working within any one group won't break any sound barriers but it also means that the group are highly unlikely to come up with any ground-breaking ideas. A good mix of personalities within any working group will always help individuals feed off each others thoughts and ideas.

Once an individual's strengths and weaknesses are highlighted it gives confidence to those whose strengths have been confirmed but also highlights the reality that there may be areas for development. If these areas for development are then dealt with a.s.a.p. by the individual's Team Leader, Supervisor or Manager where tutoring or an appropriate training course is organized then the road to success has started. It is just as important that their Team Leader, Supervisor or Manager then monitors the individual's progress. This is to ensure that what was once a weakness is now developing into a well balanced strength and that the individual is aware of the progress they are making.

The 360 degree feedback program has been proven time and time again as been a very successful and effective format when used in the helping of individuals review their own training and development needs through the eyes of their working colleagues.

The individual first completes a self-assessment which will ask them to rate themselves over a series of specific behaviours. They and their superior then select a number of working colleagues and categorise as Subordinate, Fellow Team Member, Peer, Supervisor or Manager. Each selected person then assesses the individual for their current performance under the same series of behaviours using a simple rating scale mechanism. The feedback is then summarised and collated for the individual as a series of reports. Each report is designed to emphasise a different aspect of the feedback e.g. Strengths, Development Areas, Opinion Differences. Once the individual has received the report they are then in a position to identify which behaviours are seen as in need of improvement and to choose appropriate development actions.

The 360 degree feedback program is often used as a support aid for Management Development Training. Managers can use the 360 degree feedback program report to focus on areas of the training which have been highlighted by colleagues. The 360 degree feedback report is also highly effective as a self development tool as it provides Managers with key information which they would otherwise find hard to obtain. Again I would stress that this particular tool be used only after your organization is used to and trust your present way of sourcing information for training and development needs as peoples' honesty in their views of others needs to be taken by the recipients in a mature and open minded fashion. Failure by the recipients to accept others views on them in this way could be highly damaging. The positives however, are that it can achieve a very in-depth picture of what is actually happening within any given group and will help enormously in putting together the pieces of the puzzle that will guide you in taking the right approach to training and development for everyone concerned.

If you are thinking about implementing the 360 degree feedback program for the first time within a group, it would be prudent to start with just yourself in order to allow others to view and grow comfortable with its workings and the possible benefits that can arise from such an exercise. Once others see you being comfortable with and benefiting from the program you will find that certain individuals will automatically become interested in it and may very well ask for it themselves, further solidifying its status as a truly beneficial training and development tool.

The following are two examples of basic 360 Degree Feedback Questionnaires. One is a Self-Assessment and the other a General Assessment. Both are designed to access the training and development needs of a Supervisor which should be filled out firstly by the Supervisor, then by a few peers i.e. fellow Supervisors, Subordinates and finally their Manager. These examples can be used or modified in any way to suit your own requirements, depending on the business you are in.

Example 1: Self Assessment:

360 Degree Feedback
Self Assessment

This document is being used for the sole purposes of highlighting specific training and development needs for individuals and teams as a whole. It is of utmost importance that when filling in this document that it is done so in a mature and honest manner. This will help to source and implement more adequate training material to suit the development needs of you and your group as an overall working team.

Your thoughts on questions being asked of each Skill / Competency are to be translated into Ratings of 1 (poor) – 5 (Excellent)

Date:

Name:

Position:

Department:

Skill / Competency:	Questions on Proficiency:	Rating:
Professional Behaviour	When speaking to others within your group, how would you rate your general mannerisms and behaviour towards your subordinates?	
Professional Behaviour	When speaking to people over the phone, how would you rate your phone manner?	

Professional Behaviour	When in the presence of a larger group, how would you rate your general mannerisms and behaviour towards others in general?	
Supervisory Aptitude	Overall, how would you rate yourself in your current role?	
Supervisory Aptitude	How would you rate yourself in your ability to take control of situations where a strong but calm presence is required?	
Communication Skills	How would you rate yourself in your ability to communicate well with others at all levels around you?	
Communication Skills	How would you rate yourself in your ability to effectively communicate the everyday targets and requirements to your subordinates?	
Motivational Abilities	How would you rate yourself in your ability to motivate members of your team during meetings etc?	
Motivational Abilities	How would you rate yourself in your ability to motivate individual members of your team whether meeting with them casually or as part of an official One-to-One?	

Training and Development	How would you rate yourself in your ability to train and develop individuals within your team where certain individuals might need a little more help and encouragement than others?	
Training and Development	How would you rate yourself in your ability to train and develop your team as a whole?	

Additional Information:

Is there anything that you would like to comment on or give more detail on that may help you in improving on your current level of skills and competencies?

_____

_____

_____

_____

Signed:

_____

Example 2: Assessing Others:

<u>360 Degree Feedback</u>
<u>Assessing Others</u>

This document is being used for the sole purposes of highlighting specific training and development needs for individuals and teams as a whole. It is of utmost importance that when filling in this document that it is done so in a mature and honest manner. This will help to source and implement more adequate training material to suit the development needs of you and your group as an overall working team.

Your thoughts on questions being asked of each Skill / Competency are to be translated into Ratings of 1 (poor) – 5 (Excellent)

Date:

Name of person being assessed:

Name of assessor (you):

Working relationship of assessor to person being assessed – please circle;

Subordinate - Fellow Team Member – Peer - Supervisor - Manager

Skill / Competency:	Questions on Proficiency:	Rating:
Professional Behaviour	When speaking to the assessed, how would you rate their general mannerisms and behaviour towards you as an individual?	
Professional Behaviour	When speaking to the assessed over the phone, how would you rate their phone manner?	
Professional Behaviour	When in the presence of the assessed as part of a larger group, how would you rate their general mannerisms and behaviour towards others in the group?	
Supervisory Aptitude	Overall, how would you rate the assessed in their current role?	
Supervisory Aptitude	How would you rate the assessed in their ability to take control of situations where a strong but calm presence is required?	
Communication Skills	How would you rate the assessed in their ability to communicate well with others at all levels around them?	
Communication Skills	How would you rate the assessed in their ability to effectively understand and communicate the everyday targets and requirements to their peers and / or subordinates?	

Motivational Abilities	How would you rate the assessed in their ability to motivate other members of their team, whether it be through general conversation or formal meetings?	
Motivational Abilities	How would you rate the assessed in their ability to motivate you as an individual whether meeting with the assessed casually or as part of an official One-to-One?	
Training and Development	How would you rate the assessed in their ability to understand the training and development needs required by them and those around them?	
Training and Development	How would you rate the assessed in their ability to train and develop others around them, taking into account their current role / position?	

Additional Information:

Is there anything that you would like to comment on or give more detail on that may help the assessed in improving on their current level of skills and competencies?

_____

_____

_____

_____

_____

Signed:

_____

When collating and writing the reports on the 360 degree feedback program it is important to breakdown the feedback into the following three areas - Strengths, Development Areas and Opinion Differences.

"Strengths" and "Development Areas" can in general be ascertained by how the majority of assessors perceive the assessed individual in their current role and their ability to perform their duties. This should also include their ability to positively interact with others within and outside their immediate group. "Opinion Differences" is an area which can uncover some very interesting aspects of the assessed individuals ability and behavioural patterns. It is possible that the assessed may find themselves positioned at both ends of the poor – excellent scale depending on how each assessor has benefited from and perceives the assessed individuals capability to look after them and their needs. It will also be the case that a minority of assessors will have very contrasting views on how the assessed is performing and the benefits or drawbacks they have gained from interacting with the assessed individual at different stages throughout their working life together.

When dealing with exceptions like these it is important to home in on both the positives and negatives so that the information and learning's gained from these can be better understood and then worked on. In order to fully understand these exceptions the Manager implementing the 360 degree feedback program may need to meet with certain individuals for a second time.

When trying to better understand the negative exceptions, the manager will need to ascertain whether it may be as a result of a clash of personalities or a much deeper rooted problem where the employee feels that they are being deliberately ignored, forgotten about and made feel that they are of little or no importance to their team or overall organization. If this is the case, then the Manager implementing the 360 degree feedback program must firstly find out why the assessor has come to feel like this and to gather evidence that would prove the assessors claim. Likewise, it is just as important to meet with the assessed to find out their level of awareness of the problem and why they are allowing it to develop into an exception with this particular individual. Understanding and highlighting such negative exceptions is only part of the investigation and a plan needs to be agreed mainly with the assessed in working out how this particular exception can be halted and some quality time and training given to the assessor. This should then result in the assessor feeling more confident about their own worth as an important and valued part of the overall team.

The one point I would like to make clear, is that this can be a shock to the system when going through it for the very first time. However, it will be the mature, positive and forward-thinking nature of each individual being assessed that will allow the 360 degree feedback program to bring out the best in this exercise and with it the true potential of everyone involved.

When trying to better understand the positive exceptions, the Manager implementing the 360 degree feedback program will need to ascertain as to why some of the assessed individuals abilities can be so successful and beneficial to the few but not to the majority. This is a bit different to dealing with negative exceptions in that the Manager will then have to ensure that the results of his or her findings are an intricate part of the future development of each of the assessors who made up the negative majority. It will also mean that the assessed individual will have more to do in carrying through this agreed plan as it will involve spending quality time with each of those affected. In this particular case it may be necessary that the assessed is firstly given the training and quality time that they need in order for them to better understand and follow through with the results of the feedback. It is the implementing Manager's responsibility to ensure that the assessed is given this time and knows that he or she has the support of their Team Leader while trying to bring their agreed plan to fruition.

Everyday Tips:

- Acknowledge those around you.
  (The basics such as neutral eye contact, a friendly hello or how are you? do not cost anything yet they pay huge dividends in how others will feel noticed, respected and feel like they are being appreciated and understood.)

- Supply proper Tools and Training for the Job.
  (If people cannot perform their duties due to lack of proper tools and training for the job it will kill morale and may lead to stress which in turn will lead to all kinds of problems. This needs to be in place as a basic requirement before any other advanced forms of training and development take place.)

- Keep looking at ways to boost Morale.
  (By keeping morale high in the workplace it will translate itself into a more creative and productive workforce. Again, the basics such as acknowledging others you work with, supply of proper tools and training for the job and your own approachability are just a few of the attributes that will have a huge and positive impact.)

- Ensure that Training and Development is an ongoing process.
  (To reap the rewards of true potential, it is essential that a persons training and development needs are firstly understood and then acted upon. This will lead to a more confident, competent and productive workforce.)

Leadership and learning are indispensable
to each other.

John F. Kennedy (1917 - 1963)

Speech prepared for delivery in Dallas the day of his
assassination.
22nd November 1963.

Appraisal / Review Time

Performance Appraisals / Reviews are generally held at End of Quarter or End of Year and can be daunting for both the employee and their immediate superior especially if the meeting will lead to discussions on requirements for immediate improvement followed by a poor rating for the period just ended. No one likes receiving bad news and I've rarely come across any Team Leader, Supervisor or Manager who liked giving it – those very few that seemed to relish in dishing out negativity were usually brought crashing down to earth themselves at a later stage when their own inabilities caught up with them.

In order for the Review period to work well it needs to be based on various performance aspects of an individual's overall contribution to the business as well as the results achieved. It also needs to be transparent in that it has to be based on targets (absenteeism, work rate, quality, training, contribution, involvement etc) set out the previous quarter or year. If this does not happen and the Review is loosely based on perception alone and not results orientated then it has lost credibility even before it has started. This is a hugely important time for any business and its employees and every effort has to be made in order to ensure that it is conducted and finalised in a professional manner.

There have been many debates in recent years as to the necessity of End of Quarter or End of Year Reviews and how a business could be more cost effective if they were greatly reduced or scrapped altogether. This for me is a worrying thought on a number of fronts. Psychologically it helps if people in general know that their performance over time will be reviewed and directly related to any future increases in pay conditions etc. If an organization or business cannot afford for their Supervisors and Managers to sit down for one hour with each of their subordinates every twelve weeks / six months / one year then something far more worrying is happening to the business. End of Quarter or End of Year Review time also creates the opportunity for strengthening of relationships and the Team Leader should really make use of this One-to-One meeting to allow this to happen along with discussing the review. If there is no One-to-One meeting – there is no opportunity for strengthening of working relationships.

No Surprises:

The End of Quarter or End of Year Review should mostly be comprised of two-way discussions on how to continue improving ones good points and finding mutual ways of bringing negative and disappointing points back to an acceptable level. The reality is that the individual being reviewed should nearly be able tell their superior all of this anyway as soon as he / she walks in the door. If the individual being reviewed is overly surprised, or worse still, shocked by their review meeting and the accompanying results then the previous review period has been a disaster, not necessarily from the employee perspective but definitely from a Supervisor / Manager / Business perspective. There should be no surprises in store for the individual being reviewed if the period in question was frequently complimented by good, honest and appropriate communication amongst all staff levels and continuous informal all-round feedback.

For any Team Leader capable of mastering this, then the individuals being reviewed should almost be able to give the Appraisal / Review themselves. No surprises at Review meetings will mean that there has been successful communication over a period of time up to a certain point. Continuous improvement and involvement by the individual being reviewed over further periods means that two-way communication has been a real success.

Rating or Ranking:

Oh boy, we have finally arrived at the moment of truth! Rating or ranking, rating or ranking, rating or ranking – what does one do? There have been so many heated discussions, debates and even walkouts over the past several years on which system to use and its appropriateness and fairness to either the views of those being reviewed or of the business trying to come up with a way of easily defining who it is that will benefit from the chest of money and other benefits being allocated for the upcoming financial period or year.

Let's start with Ranking. In my view, Ranking is about comparing employees with each other in a supposedly objective manner and then finally allocating each of them with a number (1, 2, 3, 4, 5,) that supposedly corresponds to whether they were more effective, the same as or less effective than their colleagues even if they were operating in different areas to those they are being ranked against. One very good example of this is where you have a number of sales people, each with their own area to operate within. The person with the best sales at the end of a given period is going to get the best rewards, the ones who are middle of the road are going to get the standard rewards and the one who is unfortunate enough to wind up with the least amount of sales will get the minimum or maybe nothing at all. Straight forward enough you might think but let's take a closer look at what drives these results and more specifically what's required to achieve them.

In this example, John, Maresa, Pauline, Catherine and Michael are the sales crew for a given company and Michael is always in top form as he is the one pulling in all the money and how his Manager is pleased with his performance. John on the other hand has a hard time keeping up with targets and spends many a long day and some evenings meeting clients in order to build up a more secure and reliable client base. The three girls are consistently meeting targets and are always very close to each other when final figures come in. Does this mean that Michael is some kind of super-hero salesman and John the worst ever salesman that was ever given a job – not necessarily so. If we look at the demographic and socioeconomic groups living within each of these areas and if we then discover that Michael has a very high percentage of his target base who are generally well-to-do and who regularly have access to disposable income, then it becomes clearer why he can succeed so easily and spend so much time living it up when others within the business are working flat out to try and achieve targets. John on the other hand works out of an area with higher unemployment statistics and where the working class families are generally more cautious about what they spend especially when mortgages have to be paid and school costs are rising. The girls operate out of very similar areas to each other and each of them put in the same amount of time and effort when working which now explains their similar results. It is also discovered that the girls put in extra time back at the office helping out in other business activities.

This example might be a bit extreme but it is a very good indicator on how wrongly employees can be evaluated when being Ranked especially on overall results alone (like sales) and does very little to take into account one of the most important factors of all – an employee's value and contribution to the overall business. What it is more likely to do in the longer term is to hinder teamwork and promote self-centred behaviours as employees will soon realise it is the only way to get rewarded.

Now let's look at Rating. Rating is firstly about comparing an employee's performance against what their Job Specification and given targets requires of them. Add to this, feedback from their superiors, peers and subordinates and how they are perceived on their communication skills, interaction skills and their general contribution to the interests of the business and those around them. If this system was used on the above sales personnel then John or one of the girls would probably be tops and for all the right reasons - John, for his tireless effort in creating a strong, long-term client base, especially within a difficult area and the girls for their flexibility in being able to contribute further skills to the running of the overall business. Michael the super-hero salesman would soon realise that the limited amount of effort it took him to achieve his results was just coincidental. He would also realise that if he were operating out of any other area he would probably be a total disaster and for his lack of contribution to the overall running and stability of the business he would loose even more points.

The Rating system, by default, helps greatly to promote teamwork, interaction, communication and contribution to the overall business. Employees who are evaluated and rewarded as such will soon realise that it is in their interest to be more proactive and that the more they learn and contribute the better their chances for further reward. This is what all organizations and businesses should really consider when looking at the pros and cons of both Rating and Ranking systems and the long-term results arising from both.

Tools for the Job:

The most important tools for the job in this particular case have to be defined and in place long before any Appraisal / Review meetings take place. These are (a) a pre-published list of objectives with reasonable targets put in place before the respective period starts. (b) One-to-One meetings which can be conducted at any time throughout the period in order to work on any performance related issues and / or other issues affecting the running of the business, and (c) Continuous and effective communication between the superior and his / her subordinates. Without these tools being in place from the start and working with some degree of credibility, a Performance Appraisal / Review is almost impossible to justify.

Assuming that the appropriate tools are in place and that all Team Leaders are proactively working with each other and their respective teams, then the End of Quarter and / or End of Year Review will be far more credible and beneficial to both the individual and the business involved.

The following are two basic examples of Performance Appraisal / Review documents - Team Member and Team Leader. These examples can be used or modified in any way to suit your own requirements, depending on the business you are in.

Example 1: Appraisal / Review document for Team Member

Performance Appraisal / Review
Team Member

Name: Review Date:

Department:

Immediate Supervisor / Manager:

Review Period: Q1, Q2, Q3, Q4, Annual,

Other (Specify) ....

This document is being used for the sole purpose of finalising and recording the overall performance results of the above individual as compared to the targets previously set out for this Review period. Results will be used to highlight, discuss and finalise future training and development needs along with the setting of various targets. This will be done in association with the setting of general performance targets and general training & development targets for the coming period as per the needs of the business. It is of utmost importance when filling in this document that it is done so in a transparent and professional manner.

Results for each Competency to be calculated as follows;
Underperformed by 20 % or more.... = 0

Underperformed by 10 – 20 % …….. = 1

Underperformed by 5 – 10 % ……… = 2

Met Target + / - 4.99 % ……………. = 3

Exceeded Target by 5 – 10 % ……… = 4

Exceeded Target by 10% or more …. = 5

	Rating: 0	1	2	3	4	5
Absenteeism – Has your absenteeism been in accordance with company policy and procedure and in accordance with the targets as set out by the Human Resource Department? Absenteeism records and other evidence may be used to clarify actual performance.						
Output – Have your overall output targets been reached taking into consideration stoppages which were beyond your control? Output and Downtime records along with other evidence may be used to clarify actual performance.						
Quality – Have your quality targets been reached taking into consideration issues not directly attributed to you? Quality charts and data along with other evidence may be used to clarify actual performance.						

Health & Safety - Have you consistently conformed to the Health & Safety policy and regulations and the targets set out by the Health & Safety Manager / Auditor? Health & Safety records along with other evidence may be used to clarify actual performance.						
Training & Development – Have you undertaken and passed all the required training and development modules as set out for this period? Training and Development records along with other evidence may be used to clarify actual performance.						

Additional Information:

Is there anything that you would like to comment on or give more detail on that would help us in gaining a better understanding of your performance?

_____

_____

_____

Details on overall scoring:

Add the points scored from each of the above Competencies and divide by the number of Competencies being rated to obtain an overall score.

Overall Rating =

*** Please note ***

There will be no pay rises or pay benefits over the next 12 months for individuals whose performances resulted in an overall rating of 0 or 1. Regular One-to-One meetings will start with immediate effect with the sole intention of giving the individuals - whose performances has failed to meet expectations - every opportunity to make an immediate and sustained improvement. Failure to obtain and sustain improvements may lead to disciplinary action being initiated with termination of contract a possibility. A Full Appraisal / Review will take place again in approx 12 weeks from this date.

There will be no pay rises or pay benefits over the next 6 months for individuals whose performances resulted in an overall rating of 2. Regular One-to-One meetings will start with immediate effect with the sole intention of giving the individuals - whose performances has failed to meet expectations - every opportunity to make an immediate and sustained improvement. Deterioration in overall performance may lead to disciplinary action being initiated with termination of contract a possibility. A Full Appraisal / Review will take place again in approx 6 months from this date where a satisfactory result will be met with appropriate pay rises and benefits.

There will be no pay rises or pay benefits over the next 3 months for individuals whose performances resulted in an overall rating of 3 or better but where there were one or more Competencies with a rating of 0 or 1. Regular One-to-One meetings will start with immediate effect with the sole intention of giving the individuals - whose performances has failed to meet expectations - every opportunity to make an immediate and sustained improvement. A One-to-One meeting in approx 12 weeks from this date will do to confirm if the performances in question have improved sufficiently. Satisfactory result will be met with appropriate pay rises and benefits.

Individuals who have met performance expectations and achieved an overall performance rating of 3 with no single Competency resulting in a rating of less than 2, will from the first day of the new financial period receive the appropriate pay rises and benefits in line with this rating.

Individuals who have met performance expectations and achieved an overall performance rating of 4 with no single Competency resulting in a rating of less than 2, will from the first day of the new financial period receive the appropriate pay rises and benefits in line with this rating.

Individuals who have met performance expectations and achieved an overall performance rating of 5 with no single Competency resulting in a rating of less than 2, will from the first day of the new financial period receive the appropriate pay rises and benefits in line with this rating.

Signed: Employee

Signed: 1st level Supervisor / Manager

Signed: 2nd level Supervisor / Manager

Example 2: Appraisal / Review document for Team Leader / Manager

Performance Appraisal / Review
Team Leader / Supervisor / Manager

Name: Review Date:

Department:

Immediate Manager / Director:

Review Period: Q1, Q2, Q3, Q4, Annual,

Other (Specify) ....

This document is being used for the sole purpose of finalising and recording the overall performance results of the above individual (including their team) as compared to the targets previously set out for this Review period. Results will be used to highlight, discuss and finalise future training and development needs along with the setting of various targets. This will be done in association with the setting of general performance targets and general training & development targets for the coming period as per the needs of the business. It is of utmost importance when filling in this document that it is done so in a transparent and professional manner.

Results for each Competency to be calculated as follows;

Underperformed by 20 % or more.... = 0

Underperformed by 10 – 20 % .... = 1

Underperformed by 5 – 10 % .... = 2

Met Target + / - 4.9 % .... = 3

Exceeded Target by 5 – 10 % .... = 4

Exceeded Target by 10% or more .... = 5

Rating:	0	1	2	3	4	5
Absenteeism – Has your own and your team's absenteeism been in accordance with company policy and procedure and in accordance with the targets as set out by the Human Resource Department? Absenteeism records and other evidence may be used to clarify actual performance.						
Output – Have your team's overall output targets been reached taking into consideration stoppages which were beyond your team's control? Output and Downtime records along with other evidence may be used to clarify actual performance.						

Quality – Have your team's quality targets been reached taking into consideration issues not directly attributed to your team? Quality charts and data along with other evidence may be used to clarify actual performance.						
Health & Safety - Have you and your team consistently conformed to the Health & Safety policy and regulations and the targets set out by the Health & Safety Manager / Auditor? Health & Safety records along with other evidence may be used to clarify actual performance.						
Training & Development – Have you and your team undertaken and passed all the required training and development modules as set out for this period? Training and Development records along with other evidence may be used to clarify actual performance.						
Professional Conduct – Have you and your team's overall professional conduct been in line with company policy and expectations as set out in the company handbook? If there were incidents of misconduct – were they dealt with accordingly and appropriately with resolution confirmed by both immediate superior and Human Resource Department? H.R. records along with other evidence may be used to clarify actual performance.						

Additional Information:

Is there anything that you would like to comment on or give more detail on that would help us in gaining a better understanding of your team's performance?

_____

_____

_____

Details on overall scoring:

Add the points scored from each of the above Competencies and divide by the number of Competencies being rated to obtain an overall score.

Overall Rating =

*** Please note ***

There will be no pay rises or pay benefits over the next 12 months for Team Leaders / Supervisors / Managers whose team's (including themselves) performances resulted in an overall rating of 0 or 1. Regular One-to-One meetings will start with immediate effect with the sole intention of giving the individuals - whose own or team's performances has failed to meet expectations - every opportunity to make an immediate and sustained improvement. Failure to obtain and sustain improvements may lead to disciplinary action being initiated with termination of contract a possibility. A Full Appraisal / Review will take place again in approx 12 weeks from this date.

There will be no pay rises or pay benefits over the next 6 months for Team Leaders / Supervisors / Managers whose team's (including themselves) performances resulted in an overall rating of 2. Regular One-to-One meetings will start with immediate effect with the sole intention of giving the individuals - whose own or team's performances has failed to meet expectations - every opportunity to make an immediate and sustained improvement. Deterioration in overall performance may lead to disciplinary action being initiated with termination of contract a possibility. A Full Appraisal / Review will take place again in approx 6 months from this date where a satisfactory result will be met with appropriate pay rises and benefits.

There will be no pay rises or pay benefits over the next 3 months for Team Leaders / Supervisors / Managers whose team's (including themselves) performances resulted in an overall rating of 3 or better but where there were one or more Competencies with a rating of 0 or 1. Regular One-to-One meetings will start with immediate effect with the sole intention of giving the individuals - whose own or team's performances has failed to meet expectations - every opportunity to make an immediate and sustained improvement. A One-to-One meeting in approx 12 weeks from this date will do to confirm if the performances in question have improved sufficiently. Satisfactory result will be met with appropriate pay rises and benefits.

Team Leaders / Supervisors / Managers whose team's (including themselves) have met performance expectations and achieved an overall performance rating of 3 with no single Competency resulting in a rating of less than 2, will from the first day of the new financial period receive the appropriate pay rises and benefits in line with this rating.

Team Leaders / Supervisors / Managers whose team's (including themselves) have met performance expectations and achieved an overall performance rating of 4 with no single Competency resulting in a rating of less than 2, will from the first day of the new financial period receive the appropriate pay rises and benefits in line with this rating.

Team Leaders / Supervisors / Managers whose team's (including themselves) have met performance expectations and achieved an overall performance rating of 5 with no single Competency resulting in a rating of less than 2, will from the first day of the new financial period receive the appropriate pay rises and benefits in line with this rating.

Signed: Team Leader / Supervisor / Manager

Signed: 1st level Manager / Director

Signed: 2nd Level Manager / Director

Everyday Tips:

- Supply of proper Tools and Training for the Job.

  (If people cannot perform their duties due to lack of proper tools and training for the job it will kill morale and may lead to stress which in turn will lead to all kinds of problems. This needs to be in place as a basic requirement before any expectations can be realistically met and other advanced forms of training and development take place.)

- Ensure that Training and Development is an ongoing process.

  (To reap the rewards of true potential, it is essential that a persons training and development needs are firstly understood and then acted upon. This will lead to a more confident, competent and productive workforce.)

- Regularly ask people about their well-being – Have they any concerns?

  (Being approachable can often uncover potential Health & Safety issues sooner rather than later. Showing a personal interest will also help you in getting to know your people)

- Have regular One-to-One meetings.

  (One-to-One meetings can be a powerful platform from which any two people can confidently and confidentially discuss their current perceptions regarding their work and the possibilities for maximising their true potential.

As the head of your respective group or team, it is important to make the most of this simple but powerful management tool which will help greatly in gaining peoples trust and resulting in a well balanced, proactive and productive team.)

- No surprises at Appraisal / Review time.
  (If the individual being reviewed is overly surprised, or worse still, shocked by their review meeting and the accompanying results then the previous review period has been a disaster, not necessarily from the employee perspective but definitely from a Team Leader / Supervisor / Manager / Business perspective. The individual going for his / her Review should in effect be almost able to give the Review themselves if all the points raised here were working successfully throughout the given period. If not, a breakdown in communication has taken place.)

Do these tips sound familiar? They should – we've explored their powerfulness in various sections throughout the book. I cannot stress strongly enough how important it is to get these competencies right in order to maximise your own and your team's effectiveness and future potential, and to do so with your team's support.

The Multicultural Workplace

Ever since the September 11th (9/11) attacks in America in 2001 and the aftermath of other terrorist attacks else where, prejudices towards certain groups of people and nationalities have been well and truly highlighted. The reality however, is that it's being happening for a very long time. Those at the receiving end of these prejudices have all too often been subject to suspicion, accusations and at times even abuse in their everyday lives. International media has done much to contribute to the problem by relaying eerie and often phobia like messages with their eye-catching headlines portraying unthinkable atrocities which may or may not have been carried out by those mentioned. What some people fail to understand is that whenever atrocities like these are carried out by whatever person or group of people it is nearly always by extremists and not by the disapproving majorities of their own kind. These majorities are just like most other groups of people around the world – hard working, family loving individuals who just want to live peaceful and harmonious lives while trying to do better for themselves and their loved ones. This is a very important point to remember when dealing with and trying to better understand a multicultural society and a multicultural workforce.

Businesses and organizations around the world that have already embraced diversity as part of their everyday working lives have long ago realised the benefits that diversity can bring to the overall scheme of things. Diversity in the workplace is like diversity in everyday life – it helps us to understand, learn and benefit from the thoughts and ideas of others we would otherwise and unnecessarily be cautious of. It can be argued that those who go through life with an unwillingness to embrace and understand diversity are often the same people who become ignorant of the benefits that diversity can bring and less interesting as individuals themselves because of it.

Do we really know what the word "Multicultural" means?

Firstly, let's look at the meaning of the word "Culture" as taken from various dictionaries;

- The totality of socially transmitted behavior patterns, arts, beliefs, institutions, and all other products of human work and thought.

- The patterns, traits, and products considered as the expression of a particular period, class, community, or population: e.g. Edwardian culture; Japanese culture; the culture of poverty; the culture of the super wealthy; French culture; American culture; small town culture; big city culture etc.

- The predominating attitudes and behavior patterns that characterize a particular group or organization.

Well, there we have it - understanding who we are as individuals, has a lot to do with where we grew up and the people we interacted with and learnt from during a particular time.

When people talk about multicultural societies they often imagine a coming together of a mixture of races and religions with different living and behavioral patterns. This can certainly qualify as being multicultural but it doesn't have to be that obvious. Anything different to your own beliefs and way of living can be classed as a variant to your own culture.

One universally familiar example of a basic form of multi-culture existence is the way in which parents and their teenage children live together, even if they don't always see "eye to eye". They may all live in the same geographical area, street and home, constantly surrounded by people they know but a simple thing like time (5, 10, 15, 20 years) can be a determining factor on why different generations of the same family may have a totally different understanding on what are acceptable and unacceptable behaviors and beliefs. Whether we realize it or not, a multi-cultural existence can often evolve from within our own homes. The question then needs to be asked why we sometimes can comfortably agree or disagree with the looks, dress sense, personal tastes, beliefs and actions of family members and friends but may hypocritically do the opposite when talking about or dealing with people of a different area, different race, different country, etc.

It is a lack of understanding of ones own cultural upbringing and how it will almost certainly differ in some aspects from that of even their own family members, friends and peers that causes certain individuals to then prejudice and even fear other types of cultures. Having the basic knowledge and understanding that we are all different in some aspects and being able to respect each others differences is a major start to living and working in a friendly and productive diversified society.

The Benefits of Diversity:

Imagine you start working in a place where your work colleagues are all exactly like you; same gender, same age, wearing exactly the same kind of clothing and believe and talk about exactly the same things you do every day of the week. This might be OK to start with (day one – hour one) but this kind of comfort zone soon turns into a place where your brain begins to shut down and you as an individual will be moved to doing anything you can to get out of a place like that because as humans it is in our nature to want to continuously seek, explore and learn about anything that is new and different.

This is how we've always improved and progressed over the centuries – by continuously looking for and learning about anything that may be different to ourselves and our current way and style of living.

The pessimists will argue that this kind of curiosity is what always gets us into trouble and is partly to blame why we have so much strife in the world. The pessimists would also prefer if the different peoples from different cultures could keep themselves to themselves, and better still, if we all lived in separate communes. A little extreme do you think? - Not to some people in the world. The reality of course is that if this did happen, the pessimists would then turn on their own communities and start finding problems with their "own kind". There will always be those who will always get worked up about the looks, habits, beliefs and behaviors of their average, everyday, run-of-the-mill neighbors and acquaintances. Thankfully the optimists out-number the pessimists in this and by default help to put a stop to this negative and backward way of thinking from taking over and unnecessarily disrupting and destroying the lives of perfectly ordinary, law abiding individuals.

The optimists as we all know, are the ones who always look at the glass as being half full as opposed to being half empty and as a result are capable of seeking out the positives and possibilities of almost every circumstance. This includes their ability and willingness to try and understand those of a different cultural upbringing to their own and especially those who live and work around them. This positive and open-minded attitude helps to unlock the true potential that a multi-cultural society or workplace can bring.

The benefits of diversity lie in the fact that we work and perform better when surrounded by people who are in some way different to ourselves and who we find interesting due to their individualism. It doesn't mean that we always agree with each others' ways or views but it does keep us interested all the same.

Whether we would like to believe it or not, diversity in any situation keeps our minds active and our brains on standby to analyze and take on any information that may be of benefit to us. The more active our minds the better the possibility that we will actively seek and use information that will be of benefit to us. This in turn is what drives our innate desire to climb ever higher on the pecking order of life.

Diversity is the key with which we can unlock the door to success. The door however, will only open if our minds are open to the opportunities and knowledge that is there for everyone to investigate and be part of.

Tools for the Job:

If you are wondering what tools can be used to help you introduce or increase diversity in the workplace, then what you should be really aiming for is the correct use of the tools you already have - just like the ones in this book. The reasoning behind this is that if you advertise for, recruit, train, develop, promote and look after all of your employees with the same non-judgmental attitude and use the tools at your disposal to seek out the individual's ability to do their job rather than holding back due to any pre-conceived concerns you may have regarding their origin or way of living, then diversity along with many other positives will flourish within your group.

You and your peers' open-mindedness, non-judgmental attitude and fairness in the development and use of various tools for the job will determine how successful you and your organization will become at creating and promoting a fair and equal base from which all employees can thrive from.

Everyday Tips:

- Acknowledge everyone with the same sense of acceptability.

  (Just like in the previous sections, neutral eye contact, a friendly hello or how are you? don't cost anything yet they pay huge dividends in how others will feel noticed, respected and feel like they are being appreciated and understood.)

- Equal and Proper use of Tools for the Job will ensure fairness and prosperity.

  (Equal and proper use of all Tools for the Job when dealing with employees will ensure that anti-diversity as an excuse, is not used by some employees who may have concerns over why they are not being awarded the same opportunities as other individuals.)

- Ability to do the job successfully comes first.
  (A person's overall ability to do their job successfully and follow procedures accordingly should be an over-riding factor in what deems an individual a valued part of any working organization, regardless of origin, etc,)

- Diversity within any group helps each member of that group feed off of each others thoughts and ideas.
  (Being able to listen to and appreciate other peoples viewpoints on any given subject is what can help individuals better understand and appreciate the meaning and complexity of those subjects.)

Emotional Intelligence

The phrase "Emotional Intelligence" was first coined by Dr. John Mayer (University of New Hampshire) and Dr. Peter Salovey (Yale University) in 1990 when they published their paper by the same name. They described Emotional Intelligence as a form of social intelligence that involves the ability to monitor one's own and others' feelings and emotions, to discriminate among them, and to use this information to guide one's thinking and actions.

It is fair to say that the paper was praised and criticized with equal intensity but unknown to everyone at the time, was the long term affect the contents of that paper would have in our everyday working and personal lives. What Dr. John Mayer and Dr. Peter Salovey did was to help us to understand how we as individuals could become more aware of our own and other peoples emotions and feelings and the knock-on affect they may have on us through our understanding and treatment of them. They also gave us an insight into how we can positively influence those emotions and feelings in order to create opportunities for ourselves.

The Mayer–Salovey model defines Emotional Intelligence as the capacity to understand emotional information and to reason with emotions. They divide Emotional Intelligence abilities into four areas.

1. The capacity to accurately perceive emotions.
2. The capacity to use emotions to facilitate thinking.
3. The capacity to understand emotional meanings.
4. The capacity to manage emotions.

They also developed a test they called MSCEIT (Mayer-Salovey-Caruso Emotional Intelligence Test) to help measure the individual's ability within each of those areas. At time of printing, this test was only available through a licensed distributor – details to follow.

Emotional Intelligence before Dr. Mayer and Dr. Salovey:

There is a strong possibility that in 50 – 100 years from now, Emotional Intelligence will be very much part of the norm and we'll all become more aware of our own and others' abilities to monitor, understand, control and influence each others emotions and feelings in order to get what we want. But hold on a minute! – Doesn't that sound familiar – I mean, how often do we give in to those around us as it is? Just think of all the people including children who just "melt us down" with their endearing smile or antics and we wind up giving them what they want anyway.

I would argue that Emotional Intelligence has always been in existence, just that we didn't fully understand it for what it was - a separate and sometimes very powerful survival tool to complement our acquired I.Q. I know that I for one, have often given in to individuals that I have had a "soft spot" for and it started long before 1990 when John and Peter first released their paper on Emotional Intelligence. What John and Peter did do, was to explain to us what exactly it is that is allowing seemingly average people to succeed far more in life and in business compared with similar people of a far higher Intelligence Quotient. There had also been several other studies done by researchers on the topic of emotional behaviour over a number of decades prior to the 1990's and they too produced results which suggested that positive emotional behaviour could have a very powerful role to play in the overall success (social & work) of those that had the ability to positively use and control it.

Attributes of Emotional Intelligence:

The five attributes that are deemed necessary to fulfil the makeup of Emotional Intelligence, are; Self Awareness, Self Regulation, Motivation, Empathy and Social Skill. Each of these attributes are important entities in their own right but when mastered and brought together at their best and most positive, will allow us to successfully use our Emotional Intelligence in the way that it is intended – to gain positive results.

Self Awareness is the basis of E.I. and if we as individuals are not aware of our own emotions and our own feelings and how they can change from time to time, then we will never understand the affects they can have on us and those we interact with.

Imagine a scenario where Eamonn is a Manager of a small group of workers and he needs his employees to try something new and different in order to see if it may be more productive. Members of the team are voicing some very negative opinions about this new approach and Eamonn is starting to get frustrated with their lack of understanding for him as their superior and their commitment to the job. He could allow this negative emotion to surface and show his frustration in front of his employees but he is also aware that this could be viewed as a sign of loosing control and makes a conscious decision to suppress it. Knowing what was happening within him and knowing what would happen if he didn't take control of it was the result of having this built-in ability of self awareness.

Self Regulation is the ability to manage one's emotions and feelings. It is the ability to be able and make a conscious decision on suppressing or stopping negative emotions from getting out of control and then allowing a more positive emotion to take its place. Just like Eamonn in the scenario when realizing that frustration was starting to take over, his self awareness told him what was happening and what would happen if it didn't stop but the ability of self regulation would allow him to control and repress the negative emotion and to allow a more positive emotion to take over. This would result in him remaining calm but just as importantly, looking calm in front of his employees.

Motivation is the ability to avoid interim temptations in order to secure greater success further down the line. Managers who possess this ability are usually forward-thinking individuals who can focus well on the actual goals presented to them and guide their teams in the necessary direction to successfully achieve those goals.

Empathy as an ability is similar in ways to Awareness and can also be described as the basis to all others. If Empathy is not present, many of the other abilities / attributes will be very difficult to come by and develop. Imagine a group of people unfortunate enough to be working for a Manager without empathy or awareness – it is like using a well bred racehorse to plough fields on a wet day. In other words, if a Manager does not have the basic ability to empathize, it will be very difficult for him or her to realize the true potential in those that they depend on.

Social Skill as an ability could be described as the sum of all the above, with the added capability of automatically monitoring and influencing the emotions of a wide range of people using a wide range of resources in order to try and secure a higher pecking order on the social or organizational ladder.

What will the Future hold?

Whatever Dr. Mayer's and Dr. Salovey's original intentions, there is one thing for sure and that is that Emotional Intelligence - as a subject to be further studied and written about - is here to stay. Human Recourse Departments and Senior Managers / Directors of various companies and organizations are paying more and more attention to this second form of intelligence and how it can best be recognised and used in conjunction with the more traditionally recognized form of I.Q.

It is possible that some time in the future, new mainstream educational techniques could be introduced that would allow students the opportunity to further study the pros and cons of Emotional Intelligence and whether or not there may be an unknown extremity that would be best left capped or exploited. How long it will take to discover the full potential of E.I., I really don't know, but if I were a betting man I would say that someone somewhere will try testing it to its limits within the next few decades. Considering the amount of books written on this subject over the past 12 years (1995 – 2007) it is hard to see the momentum stopping now and maybe we will need to revisit this subject in approx 2050 to see if true progress had actually taken place.

Tools for the Job:

Emotional Intelligence as a subject to be studied, can be very complicated especially if you intend to read and successfully decipher everything that has ever been written on it. The reason for this is that a lot of what has been written is for the most part theoretical but there is an increasing amount of tried and tested practical studies and tests which are providing some very interesting results.

There are various individuals, companies and organizations now providing the "best advice available" on Emotional Intelligence, all with their own variant on test papers etc which is why I deliberately stayed clear of trying to cover it all here in case of over-complicating it. What I hope I've done, is to present the necessary basics in Emotional Intelligence together with a few interesting parallels which together will make up an important stepping stone in further self awareness and the understanding as to why this is a subject of enormous potential for the future.

The most important aspect when researching and developing your knowledge of Emotional Intelligence is yourself combined with your long-term willingness to acknowledge, monitor and influence your own and others feelings for the sole purpose of creating positive results.

The following two websites contain a reservoir of information, guidelines and tools regarding the ongoing research into emotional intelligence by both Dr John Mayer and Dr. Peter Salovey from their respective universities.

Dr. John Mayer – University of New Hampshire
www.unh.edu/emotional_intelligence

Dr. Peter Salovey – Yale University
www.yale.edu/psychology/FacInfo/Salovey.html

You can find a growing list of individuals, companies and organizations that have developed material and test papers on the subject of Emotional Intelligence by typing in the words "emotional intelligence" into most search engines on the Internet, such as Google and Yahoo.

Everyday Tips:
- Allow yourself to tune into and be aware of your own emotions.
  (By allowing yourself to tune into your emotions or feelings you are firstly acknowledging that they exist and this is the first step in understanding the positive or negative affects these emotions can have when interacting with others.)

- Be receptive to the emotions and feelings of others.
  (Practice the ability of trying to understand the emotions and feelings of others around you and how different people in different circumstances can openly show positive and negative emotions depending on what circumstances they find themselves in.)

- Manage your emotions.
  (Once you can get to grips with understanding your own emotions, the next important step will be your ability to suppress or stop negative emotions from getting out of control and allowing a more positive emotion to take its place. Once you have mastered the ability to do this you are on your way to creating positive results for yourself through the manipulation of your own emotions and feelings – a very powerful ability.)

Work / Life Balance

Like a lot of things in life, finding that happy medium between the amount of time we spend at work and the amount of quality time we have to ourselves and with our families and friends is not always easy or possible. This is often determined by how much the corporate machine wants to extract from each of its employees together with our own understanding of, and willingness to conform to, the employer's expectation of reasonable working hours. Continuously improving on productivity is what all businesses strive for and the better the productivity the better the likelihood of increased profits. However, overworking employees on an on-going basis will only lead to some taking time off sick and / or with stress related conditions due to the negative imbalance of time spent at work trying to achieve unrealistic targets combined with the pressures being received from those at home wondering why their husband / wife / partner / father / mother / friend etc is spending less and less time with them.

Is there such a thing as a Work / Life Balance?

There is such a thing as Work / Life balance but it is mainly determined by our own understanding of what that balance should be and our individual tolerances associated with it. Being happy with the amount of time we generally spend between the workplace and at home is in the main down to personal choice and is going to be different for each individual depending on their personal circumstances. It can also be argued that the word "balance" should be seen as the balance between the employer's expectations on what they require from their workforce in order to run a profitable business and the employee's expectations on what they believe should be the maximum amount of time required of them to spend in the workplace in order for them to live a happy and contented lifestyle.

Work / Life balance has in the past been seen as a term used mainly by employees who are trying to deal with a hectic work life and who are spending less and less time to themselves and with family and friends. Work / Life balance can actually be viewed from different angles; (a) employees who would like to reduce or stabilise the amount of time they spend at work and increase or confidently define the amount of time they could spend with family and friends, (b) employers who would like to see their employees maximise the amount of time they spend at work and be able to manage their personal lives within the day or two they have off, (c) an understanding between employer and employee that both business needs and personal time are equally important, be it for different reasons, and for both employer and employee to show a willingness to support each other at times of need with the help of advance notice where possible.

Planning your Working and Personal Time:

When we look at Work / Life balance in general, there needs to be an acknowledgement and understanding of some basic ground rules from both sides of the employer / employee divide. Firstly, businesses and organisations need to understand that everyone – well, almost everyone – has a personal life with families and friends that are close to them, and when possible, would like to have the opportunity of spending quality time with them. Employees with reasonably contented personal lives perform much better at work as they'll be able to concentrate better on work related issues without the interference of negative home-life situations. It also needs to be understood by businesses and organisations that people in general go to work in order to fund a personal / home life but if employees begin to see less and less of that life due to the over-imbalance of working hours then they may very well start asking themselves questions on why they are working at all in the first place. A continuation of this kind of over-imbalance will eventually lead to negative productivity – the one thing you were trying to improve upon in the first place. Secondly, employees need to understand that without work you cannot fund a personal / home life, and family and friends need to understand that you have to be able and commit yourself for a determined number of hours each week to your employer who is paying your wages. It also needs to be understood from your own perspective and well-being that if you are not happy at work due to what you see as excess working hours and / or unrealistic working targets then it is best for everyone concerned that you discuss this with your Manager and try to come to a satisfactory resolution. It also needs to be understood that the better the business performs the more likelihood of longer term employment and hence a more secure future.

Generally speaking it is important for all businesses and organisations to understand the negative backlash that can occur from overworking employees, even those that are considered to be the most loyal and willing within the group. Continuously working your employees to the limit just because your business is booming may have a longer term negative impact on the business itself and as an employer it is wise to always keep this in mind and to do what you can to alleviate it. Like-wise it is just as important for employees to be able and show support to their employers during busy periods but also to be able and discuss with your Manager in advance the times that you may need off, be it for personal or family reasons. Again, it is in everyone's interest on both sides of the employer / employee divide to try and acknowledge and understand each others requirements and needs. This in turn will help to create as near as practically possible, the perfect balance between work and home life for everyone concerned.

Tools for the Job:

Employers need to be able determine and communicate the requirements for working hours and / or shifts for at least two weeks in advance at all times and longer if possible. Where this is not always possible then staff need to be made aware of the uncertainty of times required and as near as possible be given an estimation of worst case scenario. It is in the employers / managers own interest that all staff members have advance notice of expected working hours and the amount of time off. This will allow employees to be able spend more quality time with family and friends and for them to be able make arrangements for this in advance. It has been proven time and time again that communicating the required working hours well in advance will help the employer / manager in securing a continuous strong turnout and a reduction in absenteeism. It has also been proven in the past that a high percentage of employees are willing to support emergency situations at work where staff are asked at very short notice to stay behind in order to complete an urgent order or to catch up after a breakdown etc but it needs to be an emergency or rare occasion and not the norm.

Employees can also help by informing management well in advance or as soon as practically possible of any special requirement with regard to specific time off. This will allow management the time to organise a replacement or to re-organise workload. Employees who are generally regarded as good time-keepers and supportive of the company's goals need to be supported by the company in their time of need especially when the occurrences are few and far between.

The most important Tool for the Job here from everyone's perspective is communication, communication, communication.

Everyday Tips:

- Acknowledging and understanding Work / Life balance can help to create long term stability within the workforce.

  (Employers and Managers need to be able and communicate well in advance the required working hours for the foreseeable future. This will allow members of staff to better organise their personal lives and in turn allow them to be more committed to their work life.)

- Examine absenteeism records and discuss with regular offenders the reasons behind so much time away from work.

  (Employers and Managers may have an opportunity to reduce absenteeism within their group by finding out from regular offenders if their working pattern or the number of hours required of them at work is creating an adverse and negative affect on both the business and their personal lives.)

- Ensure that all staff are aware of the company's or organisation's overall business needs and allow for feedback on same.
  (By communicating the needs of the business to all members of staff and by allowing staff the opportunity to give feedback on time-related issues will allow for both sides to view each others requirements and hopefully arrive at a happy resolution.)

Public & Media Awareness for Managers

The term "Public and Media Awareness" is very much a generalized one and really takes into account ones continuous ability to positively present and promote themselves to their subordinates, peers, superiors, the public and the media alike. Public and media awareness is a hugely important part of any world leader's arsenal when vying for votes, come election time. Its degree of success can often be the difference between being voted in or out of office when the final result is announced. Once in power, this perception generating machine continues to work away in order to maximise the respective leader's ratings and will hopefully by default act as a "comforter" to the general public, in that they are being led by someone who is best suited for the job. It is just as important to convince those who didn't vote for that individual. Regardless of whether you are a Team Leader, Supervisor, Manager, Director or political world leader; your behaviour, body language, dress sense, words and tone of voice are just some of the ways in which positive or negative vibes can be emitted.

How you are perceived as a person and as a leader has a lot to do with how you present yourself, both within and outside your working environment. If you are continuously seen to have well defined etiquette and good behavioural tendencies then you are more than likely going to come across as being an individual of some distinction and as someone who is suited to the position of leadership. This perception is often due to the example you will set when leading your own life. It is highly unlikely that we will all become world leaders but the opening example in this chapter is a great indicator on the importance that some people in authority will place on the subject of public and media awareness and its key to their success.

Promotional Vs Negative Behaviour:

I've used the word Promotional here as apposed to the word Positive because for anyone capable of emanating continuous positive behaviour in both their working and personal lives are in fact creating the best kind of promotional advertising for themselves. This promotional behaviour has absolutely nothing to do with over-the-top "I am the best" type of behaviour, verbal communication, body language, dress-sense and / or how much drink you can take with your friends while jostling for first position on how many jokes you can get away with. That for many can actually be viewed as negative and damaging behaviour. It has however, everything to do with what's appropriate for the place and time you are in and very often how you as an individual can be singled out from a group of people as someone perceived to be of importance and / or in a position of trust even if you were doing or saying very little.

I've often come across situations where a more junior member of management or staff would often be approached for their input or opinion ahead of their immediate superior with regards to something of importance and all because of their ability to emanate continuous positive behaviour. One very good example of this is as follows; One particular company I previously worked for had a Supervisor of six months who was always very well groomed, appropriately dressed, well mannered, well spoken, approachable, professionally behaved in and outside of work and who was always helpful to others around them. This particular Supervisor was being approached on a more regular basis by Senior Management for their input into various projects and the more input they gave the more positive the perception that was being created. Within another three years this Supervisor had been promoted another two times. This Supervisor obviously had an immediate Manager, but this Manager of three years had built up an unfortunate and negative reputation of finishing projects without paying too much attention to final detail and was now starting to create an air of doubt amongst other members of management when being considered for future projects of importance. The fact that this Manager was also becoming more un-approachable over time and was beginning to lose interest in the understanding of what was considered appropriate grooming and dress sense did not help their situation either.

This is only one example of how positive promotional behaviour by anyone can be of huge importance when trying to be recognised for all the right reasons to those around them and what inevitably can happen to those who loose the interest in promoting themselves. For many of you reading this, it should automatically spark other examples of people and situations in your own working and personal lives. The reason I say this is because some people are naturally better at promoting themselves than others and especially when done in an appropriate and distinguished manner taking into account the place and the time they are in.

The long Term Affect:

Try and think for a moment about everyone you have ever known in your working and personal life and then try and think about all the famous sports stars, actors, political leaders and other celebrities you have ever seen or heard about down through the years. Now try and remember of those who were at one time highly and unquestionably respected until they made some monumental mistake, whether it was something they said or did and which forever ruined their glorious reputations and other people's perceptions of them. There are plenty of them down through the years – those we personally know and celebrities we read about in the papers - and more often than not their reputations, respectability and careers were forever tarnished. This unfortunately is the long term affect when not realising the huge importance that continuous positive behaviour can have on our lives and more so if we let continuous negative behaviour take control for the consequences can be dire and often un-changeable.

To some of you reading this it may seem a bit harsh but then again it all depends on the importance one places on their working and private lives. The more respectability that one wishes for in their life and the higher up the career ladder they want to go then the greater the fall from grace can be if they do not continuously keep in check their behavioural patterns and their ability to continuously promote themselves in a positive light to everyone else around them. It's a little bit like "Murphy's Law" – "whatever can go wrong will go wrong" – and once you are aware of this then you should also be aware of what not to get involved in, or as some might say – what not to get caught at.

Tools for the Job:

Awareness is the single most important tool you must master here. We've explored the concept and importance of awareness in a previous chapter - Emotional Intelligence –

and here is just one of the areas where you can learn to utilise and master that attribute. Be continuously aware of others around you and how you would rate them for their behaviour, verbal communication, body language and dress sense, and whether or not you would class these competencies as being appropriate for that individual considering the place and time they are in. Use this same awareness when watching T.V. or when you are at the cinema. Make a mental note of all the good or perfect examples you have encountered and work out if it is appropriate for you to mimic any of these examples in your own working and / or personal life.

Being aware of others around you does not mean that you suddenly become judgemental for all individuals have different behavioural and dress tendencies. What it does allow you to do is to work out in your own mind what you consider to be the people with the greatest ability of promoting themselves in the most appropriate and positive way and whether you can learn anything from that.

Discipline is the next most important tool you must master here. There is no point knowing how to groom, dress, behave and communicate if you are too lazy to put it into practice. If you are not already a complete natural at all of these – and very few are – then you will need to practice as often as possible until such time that you feel naturally comfortable with your new approach or until you decide that further refining and retuning needs to take place.

It's your decision – you want to make a good impression or you simply cannot be bothered. The amount of opportunities available to you over time will be determined on the choice you make.

Everyday Tips:
- Master the art of Awareness.

  (This allows you to work out in your own mind what you consider to be the people with the greatest ability of promoting themselves in the most appropriate and positive way and whether you can learn anything from that.)

- Master the art of Discipline.

  (There is no point knowing how to groom, dress, behave and communicate if you are too lazy to put it into practice.)

- Practice and Refine your skills.

  (It's your decision – you want to make a good impression or you simply cannot be bothered. The amount of opportunities available to you over time will be determined on the choice you make.)

Sources of Information

Every reasonable effort has been made to ensure that the following sources of information and associated web and e-mail addresses were correct at time of printing. If this changes for whatever reason then I suggest doing a search on the Internet to re-locate the appropriate information and the new links associated with it. The supply of third party websites and associated trademarks for informational purposes does not vest in the author or publisher any affiliation with those websites or trademarks nor does the use of such websites or trademarks imply any affiliation with or endorsement of this book by their respective owners.

The following websites can be an invaluable part of anyone's ongoing development and especially when most if not all are regularly updated to focus on the latest business techniques and / or changes in law etc.

Best Companies to Work for in the World

- U.S.A.

    www.greatplacetowork.com

- International

    www.greatplacetowork.com/international

Health and Safety in the Workplace

- European Agency for Safety and Health at Work

    http://europe.osha.eu.int

- Health & Safety Authority Ireland

    www.hsa.ie

- Health & Safety Executive UK

    www.hse.gov.uk

- Canadian Centre for Occupational Health and Safety

    www.ccohs.ca

- Occupational Safety & Health Administration USA

    www.osha.gov

- Occupational Safety and Health Service New Zealand

    www.osh.dol.govt.nz

- National Occupational Health and Safety Commission Australia

    www.ascc.gov.au

Emotional Intelligence

- Dr. John Mayer – University of New Hampshire

    www.unh.edu/emotional_intelligence

- Dr. Peter Salovey – Yale University

  www.yale.edu/psychology/FacInfo/Salovey.html

Management Training and Development

- For all Management / Development related topics

  www.everydaymanagement.com

- Free Management Library

  www.managementhelp.org

General Contact / Feedback on this Book

- For general contact, feedback and ideas towards future publications;

  E-mail: feedbackPM21C @ hotmail.com

Index

Symbols

360 Degree Program 83, 89, 90, 91, 92, 93, 97, 100, 101, 102

A

Appointments in the Media 10
Appraisal / Review 107, 109, 113, 114, 117, 119, 122, 123, 126
Awareness 14, 16, 17, 27, 29, 33, 48, 76, 101, 138, 139, 141, 151, 152, 155, 156

B

Best Companies to Work for 160
Branding. *See* Recruiting

C

Choosing the Right Candidate 25
Constructive Criticism 52

D

Discipline. *See* Public / Media Awareness
Diversity 12, 128, 132, 133
Dr. Mayer. *See* Emotional Intelligence

E

Effective Communication 51
Efficiency 5, 6
Emotional Intelligence 8, 25, 141, 142
Equal Opportunity 12
Everyday Tips 26, 48, 72, 102, 125, 133, 142, 148, 157

F

Famous Quotes 105

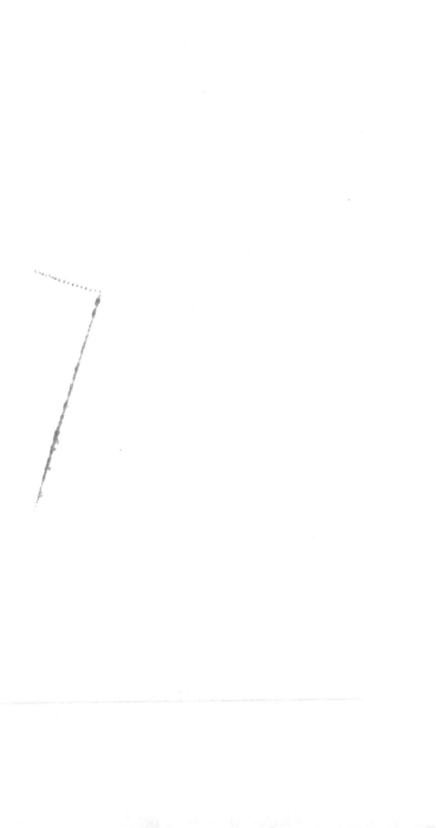

Printed in the United Kingdom
by Lightning Source UK Ltd.
125044UK00001B/196/A